How to Check Out Your Competition

How to Check Out Your Competition

A COMPLETE PLAN FOR INVESTIGATING YOUR MARKET

John M. Kelly

JOHN WILEY & SONS

New York · Chichester · Brisbane · Toronto · Singapore

Library of Congress Cataloging in Publication Data:

Kelly, John M.
  How to check out your competition.

  Bibliography: p.
  1. Competition. 2. Marketing research.
3. Corporate planning. 4. Competition, International.
I. Title.

HD41.K537   1987   658.8'02   86-32408
ISBN 0-471-85670-3 (pbk.)

Printed in the United States of America

10 9 8 7 6 5 4 3

Preface

In recent years more than 60,000 businesses in the United States went bankrupt. They included both start-up concerns and long-established companies. They failed for all kinds of reasons—poor management, declining markets, inept marketing, inefficient manufacturing. But all these companies shared a single characteristic—they were not able to compete in the marketplace.

If your company is destined to grow and prosper rather than follow these less fortunate firms into obscurity, it needs to be able to win in the competition that takes place in every market. You have to do more than manage your business well—you have to manage it better than your rivals manage theirs. You have to identify what constitutes a competitive advantage in your industry, then make sure that your company has that advantage.

The purpose of this book is to make you the most effective competitor in your business. Reading it and filling in the Competitive Analysis Worksheets will give you an in-depth understanding of the competitive dynamics of your market. It will show you the strengths and weaknesses of each of your principal competitors. And it will suggest specific actions you can take right now to move your company into a stronger competitive position.

With the superior business information system outlined in *How to Check Out Your Competition* you will:

Chart more profitable corporate strategies based on competitive insights

Uncover and exploit vulnerable points in competitors' operations while erecting strong defenses in your own

Avoid profit-draining surprises from aggressive rival firms

Build market share by capitalizing on areas your competition will not or cannot move into

Protect against information overload with a system that collects all of what you need and only what you need

Save countless hours of frustration and fruitless digging for facts by your managers, your staff, and yourself

The book is designed as a "turnkey" system. If you already have a competitor analysis effort, it will tell you how to make it more effective, how to organize it, and how to make sure it is giving you the insights you need. If you don't engage in any systematic competitive analysis now, *How to Check Out Your Competition* will show you—in a step-by-step manner—how to establish a system, how to compile basic information files on competitors, how to analyze your markets, how to disseminate information to decision makers, and especially how to integrate competitor analysis into the actions that your company is taking right now.

The male personal pronoun *he* is used throughout the book strictly for the sake of convenience and readability; it should be read to include women as well as men.

John M. Kelly

New York, New York
March 1987

Contents

Contents

Contents

How to Check Out Your Competition

1

Injecting a Competitive Approach in Your Planning Process

Our market growth is not outstanding, so we've got to go out and take market share away from our competitors.

CARL E. PFEIFFER
President Quanex Corp. (a steel company)

Robertshaw and our competitors are operating in a worldwide market-place where traditional patterns no longer apply. . . . New competitors are clawing at the door—and some have broken through.

RALPH S. THOMAS
President, Robertshaw Controls Co.

These statements typify what many business leaders are saying today: Competition is fierce. Markets are no longer booming. Success depends on finding ways to make gains at the expense of competitors. Survival depends on anticipating the actions of rivals to effectively defend your market share.

Competitor Orientation

Business theorists have identified three different phases of management orientation. The first was *product orientation.* Henry Ford's Model T, the early days of Polaroid, Xerox, or IBM—in all these cases the emphasis was on what was being sold, on production methods, on technical innovation. The successful firms had desirable products, were able to produce quality products for a relatively low price, and effectively applied technology.

Gradually, though, many managers changed their thinking. They emphasized greater responsiveness to the market. Management consultant Peter Drucker declared that the basic goal of all businesses was "to create a customer." This *customer orientation* meant finding better ways to serve customers' needs, examining what customers could use rather than trying to sell them what you produced. Products were still important. But more important was the focus on the functions they fulfilled, the search for further unmet needs.

IBM, General Electric, 3M, and many other companies adopted this orientation and prospered. It opened the way to new opportunities. It seemed the ideal way to run a business, partly because many markets were expanding rapidly. The long post-World War II boom meant that most firms could grow simply by participating in growth markets. If total sales were increasing 20 percent each year and new realms of customer needs were opening up regularly, there seemed to be no sense in worrying about the plans of competitors, or about gaining a few points of market share.

Another Change

In the past decade, a new mode of thinking has emerged. Growth in many industries has slowed. Booming markets have matured. To grow, most companies can no longer "ride the market." Astute managers have adopted a new approach. They see success or failure in terms of winning the struggle with competitors—for market share, for personnel, for technological advancement, for resources.

Just as customer orientation included attention to products, *competitor orientation* requires that care be given to both products and customers. But quality products and efficient service of customers' needs are only elements of a competitive approach. They are two possible sources of competitive advantage, but not the only two.

Process innovation, access to financing, marketing skill, efficient distribution, cost control—all these are sources for obtaining an edge over rivals. In all three schools of thought, winning customers is the ultimate goal. But competitor orientation looks beyond just satisfying customer needs and views the customer as the prize in a multifaceted struggle with competitors.

A Zero-Sum Game

In a zero-sum situation, what one party wins, another party loses. Customers are in limited supply. As a result, what counts in the market "game" is not just how well you do, but what your performance is relative to that of your competitors. Your costs, your sales efforts, your product quality—all have to be judged in relation to the competitors' business.

You can no longer just ask the traditional customer-oriented questions: What do they want? Which customer segments are growing? Why are they satisfied or dissatisfied with our products? You now have to ask competitor questions:

Which competitors pose a threat to us?
From which competitors are we taking market share?

How can we protect our market sectors?

How are competitors vulnerable to our moves?

What Is Competitive Analysis?

Competitive analysis (interchangeable with competitor analysis) is a basic tool of business that takes a competitive approach to the market. While it involves collecting competitor information, it is not fundamentally a data-gathering exercise. Rather, it is a process by which you can understand your competitors. What are they doing? What are they planning? How might they carry out their plans?

Some managers don't think they can ever really gain a thorough knowledge of the operations and thinking of their competitors. Their philosophy is, "I'll know what he's going to do when he does it." The problem today is that if you wait to react to competitive moves after they are revealed, you will find yourself steadily falling farther behind in the struggle.

Competitor analysis enables you to anticipate moves. It lets you both plan defenses of your territory and prepare for opportunities that result from competitor mistakes and weaknesses.

Essentially, competitor analysis serves five purposes:

1. **Holding Market Share.** Your competitors are planning to lure your customers away. How will they do it? Are their products better suited to the customers' needs? Are they cheaper? Are they marketed better? Is the competitor taking advantage of new technology? New sales strategies?
2. **Increasing Your Market Share.** The only way to do this in many cases is to attract customers away from your rivals. How can you do so? Where is the competitor vulnerable? Do you have a competitive advantage that you are not fully exploiting? Is your competitor weak in his advertising? Is the structure of his business a market handicap?

3. **Learning His Strengths and Weaknesses.** Maybe your competitor is experiencing a cash-flow problem. Maybe he is weak in marketing. Production difficulties may be delaying deliveries. You cannot take advantage of his weaknesses unless you know about them. Competitor analysis brings together isolated bits of information and presents you with a picture of exactly where the competitor is strongest and where he is vulnerable.

4. **Preparing for Contingencies.** In business, surprises are rarely enjoyable. New technology, altered product designs, substitute materials, new competition—these can appear on the scene at any time and disrupt your plans without warning.

5. **Learning from Competitors.** The detailed view of competitors' operations that you obtain allows you to identify the most effective aspects of their businesses in order to use them to your advantage. This may include new technology, a novel way of compensating salespeople, or an innovation in tooling. You can see what works for him—and what doesn't. It will be less expensive to learn from his mistakes than from your own.

An Ongoing Process

Competitive analysis is a method to monitor change. As such it can't be an isolated event, but must be a continuing process. This means:

Assigning ongoing responsibility for the function to a specific manager.

Making competitor analysis a part of your planning process.

Filling in the Competitive Analysis Worksheets on a regular basis, plus conducting competitor reviews in response to unexpected developments.

Constant efforts to keep all employees "competitor conscious" so that they are alert to any significant competitor information they encounter and incorporate competitive thinking into their jobs.

From Analysis to Action

Your principal competitor introduces a substantial price reduction on an important product. You are suddenly faced with a decision. Should you match his price to hold your market share? Should you do nothing, assuming he will have to raise his price again before many of your customers switch? Should you enhance other inducements associated with the product such as including a longer warranty? Should you step up your sales or advertising efforts?

Before you can make an informed decision, you need to know some things about the competitor. Has he introduced a process innovation or some other measure that gives him a lower cost? Does he have the financial resources to sustain a prolonged price war? Is he trying to liquidate inventories in order to solve a temporary cash-flow problem? Is he aiming to become the low-price leader in the market? Has he lowered the quality of his products in order to be able to sell them for a lower price? What is the long-term strategy of the company's executives? How might they react to the counteractions you are contemplating?

Competitor analysis is designed to give you the answers to these pressing questions so that you can decide on a course of action. In fact, with an ongoing competitive analysis system, you will already have a good idea of the competitor's operations, the quality of his products, his cash-flow picture, his financial resources, and the thinking of the firm's executives. You may even have anticipated the price cut and been ready in advance to take appropriate action.

Always make an effort to turn competitive analysis into specific action. Feed the data you collect directly into your decision-making process. Think about the issues raised in the Information Keys and Action Probes scattered through the book.

2

Why You Need Systematic Competitive Analysis

Too many companies neglect competitive analysis or consider it of secondary importance. "I have enough problems running my own business," executives say. "Why should I worry about what my competitors are doing?"

In addition to the pressure of day-to-day concerns, this reluctance to initiate organized competitor analysis is often reinforced by the following attitudes. Make sure your company doesn't suffer from them.

Attitudinal Barriers

Complacency. Success can make you rest on your laurels until you are suddenly faced with tough competitive pressures that you're not prepared for. Johnson & Johnson, a sophisticated and successful marketer of consumer products, invested heavily a few years ago in disposable diapers. Just as the company prepared to sit back and collect the profits on its conventional, premium-priced product, two competitors—first Procter & Gamble, then Kimberly-Clark—introduced elastic diapers in the same price range. Johnson & Johnson, with no comparable product, had to leave the field, decidedly poorer.

It Can't Happen Here. "My industry is stable. Major changes in the competitive climate are impossible." This notion can be fatal.

> The slide ruler market was stable—until the electronic calculator made the product obsolete overnight.

> The bicycle market was stable for years—until new designs, materials, and trends opened significant opportunities for the companies, like Huffy and Ross, ready to take advantage of them.

> The U.S. auto market had settled into a very stable pattern—until importers changed the rules of the game and drove major U.S. companies to the brink of bankruptcy.

The only rule that doesn't change is that every industry does change. What could your competitors or potential competitors be doing right now that will mean trouble for you tomorrow? Shouldn't you find out?

I Don't Want to Hear It. Some executives shy away from competitive analysis because they dread the chore of wading through piles of data and trying to figure out what it all means. They find the task confusing.

One purpose of an organized competitive analysis program is to eliminate this information overload. Once you've recognized the key factors of competitive success in your industry, once you've learned to distinguish quality of information from quantity, and once you know how to compile and arrange data systematically, you'll find that important competitor information will become clearer, that all the pieces of the puzzle will fall into place.

We Have the Information Already. Your salespeople know what's going on in the market. Your research and development people follow technical developments. Why make it more complicated?

The parable of the blind men and the elephant applies here. One man felt the elephant's leg and said an elephant is like a tree. Another felt the tail and claimed an elephant resembled a rope. A third felt the trunk and swore an elephant was like a snake.

What you want to see is the whole elephant. Your salespeople may observe a competitor move aggressively in price. But your financial manager might determine that he's strapped for cash and that the price drop will be temporary. And one of your engineers may tell you that a new material the competitor has introduced will give him a cost advantage and that his prices have to be taken seriously.

A coordinated, organized, and ongoing competitive analysis effort enables you to assemble these bits of information into a coherent and revealing whole.

Assumptions. Success breeds complacency, but even struggling companies are subject to unexamined assumptions. The worst assumption is often that a competitor will do things the way you do.

For instance, many toy manufacturers have traditionally assumed that their business has to be highly seasonal, structured around the Christmas buying season. Mattel, a strong competitor in the field, has recently begun efforts to spread sales over a large part of the year, increasing manufacturing efficiency and capturing market share. Competitors' assumptions left them unprepared to respond.

Competitive analysis questions assumptions. It helps you anticipate surprises. It shows you the real landscape of your industry, with all its pitfalls and opportunities.

Ten Reasons Why You Need a Competitive Analysis Program

1. To Survive. Twenty years ago, Harley-Davidson, the only U.S. motorcycle manufacturer, welcomed the expansion of Japanese participation into the market. Harley-Davidson planners thought the newcomers would stimulate demand for all makes of motorcycles. Failing to accurately investigate and analyze the competitors' motives, Harley-Davidson neglected to take any effective steps to protect its market. Honda, Suzuki, and others, though, had no intention of confining themselves to the low-end segment that they'd initially entered. They eventually offered a full range of products, including large motorcycles, striking at the heart of Harley-Davidson's market. Harley-Davidson's sales and profits were hit hard. And while the company remains in business, the damage that it suffered has been severe. Competitive analysis can be a question of life or death for your company.

2. To Handle Slow Growth. Companies realize that their markets are no longer booming. The world economy has recently been beset by a pattern of stagflation, recession, and weak recovery. Positional strategy—riding the market—is no longer good enough. To grow, you need to grab market share. To survive, you need to protect your current share from competitors looking to grow at your expense.

If your industry is still growing today, all you have to do is look at a few that are more mature than yours. Cigarettes, beer, major appliances— all have reached states of slow growth or no growth. What character-izes these markets? Intense competition for share.

And the change from growth to stagnation can happen quickly. Armour, once the fourth largest company in the United States, fell into eclipse in the 1960s as the growth in meat consumption leveled off. Failing to foresee the development, Armour faltered and was acquired.

3. To Cope with Change. RCA was once a big factor in the vacuum tube business. When solid-state electronics took over, the company failed to keep a close enough watch on the way competitors were reacting to the change. While Sylvania and Raytheon found niches in which they could gradually and profitably wind down their operations, RCA was forced to take a major write-off.

Technological innovations, new products, alternate materials, new ways of distributing, new manufacturing methods—change continually affects every industry. Steel companies suddenly have to deal with competition from lower-cost minimills. Air freight forwarders have had to adjust to competitors offering overnight service. Competitor analysis will keep you abreast of change, and even a step ahead of it. Its focus is anticipation, contingency planning, preparedness—qualities that are needed in business today more than ever before.

4. To Cash in on Opportunities. The Japanese have few roads, an efficient public transportation system, and a small domestic automobile market. They are a long distance from major U.S. and European markets. They possess minimal natural resources. Yet by spotting and carefully analyzing an opportunity in the world auto market, this nation's producers have overcome all obstacles and succeeded in making Japan the world's largest maker of automobiles. In the process, they have overtaken many powerful, entrenched competitors.

This is probably the most vivid example of the potential that effective competitor analysis holds for every company and every industry. Not only can it help you to react to change and defend your market, it can show you how to manage change to your advantage and make the best of every market opportunity.

5. Because Success Is Not Enough. You may be doing an excellent job in many areas of your business. The problem is, how well you do isn't the ultimate test. What counts is your *relative* performance. You may have an efficient plant, but a competitor's may be more efficient. Will he be able to attract your customers with a lower price and still turn a profit? Your product development effort may appear effective. But if your competitors consistently top you in bringing new products to the market, how long will you hold your share?

No internal measure can determine relative success. No matter how extensive your system of controls and evaluation, only by examining your performance in relation to that of your competitors can you determine precisely where you stand.

6. To Uncover Key Factors. What is it that distinguishes success from failure in a specific industry? What really matters? Which factors are important, which inconsequential?

One company may prosper because of its effective sales organization, another because it has an efficient plant. Service may be the key to success, or product design. Competitor analysis enables you to pinpoint exactly what the successful companies in your industry are doing right—and what the losers are doing wrong. It focuses your strategic planning and the efforts of your entire organization on these key factors.

7. For Multiple Rewards. Competitor analysis offers more than just a look at what your rivals are doing. By focusing your attention on key factors and relative success, your competitive analysis program will help *all* managers do their jobs better.

Almost every manager competes. A personnel director competes in the labor market for the best employees. A purchasing manager competes for the most favorable terms from suppliers, and sometimes for access to scarce materials.

The personnel director knows he's doing a good job if his company is competing well—if it's hiring better engineers than other firms in the industry, or if turnover is lower. But to determine this, he has to analyze what the competitors are doing. The same applies to almost every function in your business.

. . . .

A Winner That Knows Its Battlefield

Caterpillar Tractor is a good example of a company attuned to key competitive factors. The company's managers realized long ago that reliability is essential in the heavy equipment field. If a bulldozer breaks down, a contractor can lose thousands of dollars a day.

As a result of this recognition, Caterpillar has always emphasized quality and durability in its products. In addition, it has reached for a competitive edge by establishing an extensive dealer and service network. The company promises to deliver virtually any replacement part anywhere in the world within 24 hours. If the part doesn't arrive in 48 hours, it's free.

The result: Caterpillar has become the leading construction equipment manufacturer in the world and commands a premium price for its products.

Other companies can learn a lesson in key factors from Caterpillar's experience. Price, advertising, or superficial design characteristics are not likely to lead to success in this business. Competitors must first address the key factors of quality and service. Komatsu, Ltd., a Japanese heavy equipment maker now trying to increase its market share, has done just that. It has succeeded by patterning its approach to the business on Caterpillar's.

. . . .

8. To Reinforce Intuition. Most executives have a "feel" for their industry. Experience and informal information gathering enable you to read your market and "guess" what your competitors are doing or are going to do.

But intuition can never take the place of in-depth analysis. Pharmaceutical companies felt sure that customers wouldn't turn heavily to cheaper generic drugs. But now they face slipping profits as generics expand rapidly. No matter how good your feel for your market, you still need adequate analysis based on current and reliable information.

9. To Improve the Quality of Your Decisions. Managing a business means making a series of decisions. If you are to reach your goals, your decisions must be based on realities. Competitive analysis gives you information about the current alignment of forces in your market.

In addition, it provides valuable insights into the determinants of success and failure.

Experience is expensive. Xerox paid heavily for its unsuccessful attempt during the 1970s to enter the computer market—and no doubt learned a good deal in the process. Another office products company could learn many of the same lessons in a much less costly way; that is, by keeping close track of what Xerox was doing and analyzing the reasons for its failure.

10. To Stay Competitive. Imagine the executives of your strongest competitor sitting in the boardroom discussing your company. They've examined the background and experience of your key executives. They've tracked the type of people you've been hiring. They've obtained credit reports on your finances. They know your plant capacity and a great deal about your capital spending plans. They've reverse-engineered your products. They've gleaned information from your suppliers and your customers. Now they're formulating plans to increase their market share at *your* expense.

A final reason you must embrace competitive analysis is because you have to assume that your competitors are doing it to you. They're looking for your weaknesses. You can't afford to wait until the attack begins. You must get to know their strategies, their resources, and their weaknesses now. If you don't, you'll be in a poor position to defend yourself, to counterattack, to compete.

Surveying Current Competitive Analysis Capabilities

You must introduce a systematic competitive analysis program in your company in which:

The effort is highly directed and efficient

The program is action oriented

The program involves and benefits a wide range of managers

To accomplish these goals, you should begin by looking in detail at the competitor analysis capabilities you have now.

Competitive Analysis Worksheet 1 will help you take a close look at your current situation. It will pinpoint your strengths and weaknesses in competitive analysis and give you a picture of the base on which you can begin to build your program.

If your business is divided into distinct product lines, plants, or divisions, you should duplicate the sheet and fill in one copy for each segment. Your answers to Part B will require you to poll department heads responsible for various functions. This is a good time to seek input from them on competitive analysis contributions and needs.

COMPETITIVE ANALYSIS WORKSHEET 1

PRELIMINARY COMPETITIVE ANALYSIS SURVEY

Completed by _____   Date _____

Plant/division _____

Part A

1. What overall role does competitive analysis play in your company/division? (check one)

   ____ Essential   ____ Sporadic   ____ Marginal   ____ None

2. Is competitor data used in strategic planning?

   ____ Yes   ____ No

3. Are competitor reactions taken into account in major tactical moves such as product introductions?

   ____ Yes   ____ No

4. Has any person or department been given responsibility for the central collection or analysis of competitive information?

   ____ Yes   ____ No

5. What person or persons, if any, are most directly involved in current competitor analysis?

   Person _____   Dept. _____

   Person _____   Dept. _____

6. Is competitive information from various sources consolidated?

   ____ Yes   ____ No

7. Have employees been instructed how and why to report all relevant information on competitors?

   ____ Yes   ____ No

8. Have you conducted competitor analysis projects on an ad hoc basis (e.g., before a plant expansion)?

____ Often   ____ Sometimes   ____ Rarely   ____ Never

9. How successful was this ad hoc research?

____ Satisfactory   ____ Unsatisfactory

10. Do you plan to increase sales in the foreseeable future?

____ Yes   ____ No

11. What are your projected sales increases over the next two years?

Year 1: ____%

Year 2: ____%

12. Will this growth come primarily from new customers, from customers you attract from competitors, or from both?

____ New customers   ____ Competitors' customers   ____ Both

13. If you plan to attract customers from competitors, how will you do this?

_____

_____

_____

14. If you plan to increase market share, have you considered how individual competitors might react to your tactics?

____ Yes   ____ No

15. Have you lost customers or market share to competitors in the past?

____ Yes   ____ No

In what products/market areas?

_____

_____

_____

16. Have you analyzed why these customers switched to competitors?

           ___ Yes   ___ No

17. Are competitors leaving or entering your major market?

       ___ Leaving   ___ Entering

18. Why are they doing so (e.g., high profit margins, mature market, foreign entrants, etc.)?

_____

_____

19. Is your business more or less competitive than it was five years ago?

     ___ More   ___ Less   ___ Same

20. Do you expect it to be more or less competitive five years from now?

     ___ More   ___ Less   ___ Same

21. In what areas has competition particularly heated up, and in what areas do you expect it to increase?

	Has Increased	Will Increase
Pricing	___	___
Marketing	___	___
Products	___	___
Technology	___	___
Sales	___	___
Labor	___	___
Manufacturing	___	___

22. The following factors tend to increase the urgency of competition in an industry. Which ones apply to your business?

	Applies	Does Not Apply
Slow market growth	___	___
Commodity business	___	___
Minimal differentiation	___	___
Foreign competitors	___	___
Diverse competitors	___	___
Mature market	___	___
Technological change	___	___

Part B

What role does competitive analysis play in each of the following areas of your business:

Function	Level of Competition (Intense/ Average/ Light/None)	Position of Your Company's Performance among Top Five Competitors	Competitive Analysis is a Factor in Decision Making (Always/ Sometimes/ Seldom/Never)
Purchasing	_____	_____	_____
Personnel	_____	_____	_____
Salary	_____	_____	_____
Production	_____	_____	_____
Marketing (general)	_____	_____	_____
Promotion	_____	_____	_____

Function	Level of Competition (Intense/ Average/ Light/None)	Position of Your Company's Performance among Top Five Competitors	Competitive Analysis is a Factor in Decision Making (Always/ Sometimes/ Seldom/Never)
Advertising	_____	_____	_____
Sales	_____	_____	_____
Pricing	_____	_____	_____
Strategic planning	_____	_____	_____
Finance	_____	_____	_____
Research and development	_____	_____	_____
New products	_____	_____	_____
Service	_____	_____	_____

3

Advance Planning for a Competitive Analysis Program

Your goal for developing a competitive analysis program is to maintain and improve your competitive position in every facet of your business. To accomplish that goal, you must begin by conducting a three-step evaluation of your current competitive position. First, examine your own company, the business you're in. Second, scrutinize your customers and their needs. Third, identify the key factors in your industry or market.

This planning effort will give you a very precise idea of the direction your research and analysis should take. After you've begun to collect competitor and market information, you can go back and develop an even sharper focus on these matters. But a preliminary survey is needed to guide your search and research.

Defining Your Business

"What is our business?" This is a question that may seem simple and obvious, but that actually requires a great deal of careful consideration. Too few executives give it enough thought. Competitive analysis begins with this question because the answer determines how you compete, who you view as a competitor, and what you see as the key factors in your analysis.

Take, for example, Eastman Kodak. The firm pioneered amateur photography with the Brownie camera and its many successors. You might conclude that Kodak's business is selling cameras. But look more closely. Kodak makes far more money selling film and film processing than it does cameras. It always has. Camera sales, in fact, are primarily a means of promoting film sales rather than an end in themselves.

Kodak executives have always recognized this. Has it shaped the way they compete? Definitely. Kodak has become the dominant force in all areas of the film market, currently accounting for 85 percent of film sales in the United States. It has actively defended this "turf" (market) against all competitors.

However, the company has taken a different approach to the camera market, even yielding segments—35mm cameras, for example—to competitors. Why? Because Kodak is in the film business. A Nikon camera buyer is another potential user of Kodak film.

A similar definition might apply to a maker of industrial grinding machines. Rather than saying, "Our business is manufacturing and selling machines," management at such a company might decide, "We're in the abrasives business." Machine buyers would then be seen primarily as customers for replacement grinding wheels, abrasives, and related products. Competitive focus would be on ways to defend market share from other abrasives producers.

What is the business of a department store? If a retailer defines his business as "serving as a middleman between manufacturers and customers," then he is likely to develop a particular competitive focus. He may concentrate on the logistics of supply, store location, and depth of inventory. He's also likely to lose business to more aggressive competitors who take a different view.

"Retailing is show business" is an old saying in the industry. This definition dictates a different competitive emphasis than the middleman attitude. Macy's, the New York City-based chain of department stores, organizes an enormous Thanksgiving Day parade to start the Christmas selling season. It sponsors fireworks displays and is known for its in-store demonstrations and celebrity visits. None of these has to do with its middleman role. All have to do with *show business.* And they have helped Macy's to prosper while less imaginative competitors—such as rival E. J. Korvettes—have fallen by the wayside.

Polaroid was forced to ask the business definition question when the expiration of its instant photography patents brought about a new competitive situation. Rather than saying its business was cameras or film, Polaroid executives decided the firm was in the imaging business. This led to a major research effort in the emerging field of electronic imaging and set a new direction for the company.

Robert Vlasic realized that most pickle company executives saw their business as manufacturing pickles. He defined his company's business as marketing a particular food product. Pickle making became a means, not an end. Vlasic was able to win considerable market share by focusing on marketing and promotional factors such as the creative use of advertising.

A trio of actual definitions used by companies today is shown below.

. . . .

Three Actual Business Definitions

Hercules Incorporated is a supplier of a broad line of natural and synthetic materials and products and related systems. The company serves a broad range of industries around the world, including the electronics, packaging, aerospace, food, synthetic fibers, automotive, graphic arts, adhesives, paper, coatings, and personal-care industries. Its fundamental strength is its technological heritage, which enhances the development and marketing of products and systems to meet growing customer needs.

CTS Corporation is primarily in the business of designing and manufacturing electronic components and subsystems for original equipment manufacturers (OEMs) in the electronics industry.

The Dunkin' Donuts concept is to make and sell the freshest and most delicious coffee and donuts and related bakery products, served quickly and courteously in sparkling clean, well-merchandised shops.

. . . .

The Corporate Mission

Slightly different, but equally important, is the broader question of corporate mission. Theodore N. Vail, who was head of AT&T during its early days, once stated that "our business is service." While this did not specifically define AT&T's business, it established a value that guided the company's efforts for many years. It led both to the advanced technology needed for the best service, and to a continuing emphasis on service in operations. It helped AT&T to become the dominant phone company in the United States.

Executives of IBM, another progressive corporation, long ago decided that the company's mission was not to manufacture and sell computers, but to solve data storage, retrieval, and processing problems. This sense of mission has had a great deal of impact on how IBM competes, which markets it enters, how it approaches technology and service, and what it views as key factors in its industry. It has led to the *systems* approach, which has been an important factor in IBM's market power.

In 1932, Konosuke Matsushita, founder of the Matsushita Electronic Industrial Co., laid down for his company the principle of *meichi* or "realization of mission." He stated that the company should manufacture high-quality but reasonably priced goods in an effort to contribute to the peace, prosperity, and happiness of society. He eschewed profit for its own sake and inferior products of any kind.

This *meichi* has guided Matsushita to become a highly successful and very competitive company. In fact, the concept of zero-defect products helped Matsushita and other Japanese manufacturers break into the U.S. electronics markets without the expense of establishing extensive service networks like those possessed by American rivals.

Company Niche

An important theory in biology is Gause's principle of mutual exclusion, which states that "no two competitors can coexist who make their living in the identical way." The idea holds true in business as it does in nature. The most successful companies are always striving to find or reinforce their unique niche.

Your niche may be defined geographically. A coal company in one region may produce the same grade of coal as one in another, but each will service its local geographic area. Wholesalers, retailers, distributors, hotels, construction companies, and many other firms traditionally define their niches primarily on a geographic basis.

A niche can also be defined by product attribute—latex versus oil paint—or by method of distribution—mail order versus retail store— or simply by customer perception—brand name versus generic.

Knowing your niche is an important step in preparing for competitor analysis. It clarifies the territory you must defend. And looking at the market in terms of niches can spotlight opportunities as well as warn about the need to defend yourself. Marriott Corp. identified two distinct niches with potential in the hotel business—upscale business lodgings and medium-priced "courtyard" hotels. The company has moved into both areas while avoiding such overcrowded niches as casino hotels.

Your Company's Measures of Success

Another crucial question to ask about your company is "How do we measure success?" The answer influences the way you view competitors. The company that measures success mainly in terms of sales growth will take an aggressive stand regarding competitors, fighting hard to win new customers and to hold current ones. A firm whose main criterion is return on assets will be less interested in holding onto customers at any price. Maintaining an unstained image and serving the community may be an important measure of success for one firm, while another will concentrate on maximizing investors' income.

Most businesses have more than a single measure of success. Maybe your first reaction will be that profits are your only measure. But careful consideration will show that your real yardsticks are liquidity, market share, or level of employment.

Once you've identified your prime measures of success, ask whether they're appropriate for your competitive climate. James Ling established growth through acquisition as a vital criterion at his conglomerate Ling-Temco-Vaught (Now LTV Corp.). He "succeeded" by moving the company from being the 204th largest U.S. industrial concern in 1965 to being the 14th largest four years later. But 1969 also saw the firm lose more than $38 million and marked the beginning of a precipitous decline. Ling's measure of success turned out poorly.

Analyzing Your Customers

The next step in this preplanning stage is to take a close look at your customers. Since customers are usually the most important prize in the competitive struggle, it's important to know who they are and what their needs are.

Who are they? The answer to this question cannot be obtained from a buyers' list. Look closely at who makes the *decision* to purchase your product or service. For example, most beer in stores is bought by women, but men decide the brand in almost all cases. Who is the customer? Supermarket shoppers purchase laundry detergent, but the store manager decides which brands are displayed and how much space each is given. He may be the soap company's primary customer.

Recognizing the customer is a key to mapping competitive strategy. Appliance makers like General Electric and Whirlpool have included home builders as a major segment of their customer base. Maytag has used a different competitive tactic, selling only through retail stores. Each definition of customers has its advantages and each helps set the competitive stance of the company involved.

What Does the Customer Purchase?

A company in the oil field supply business was being considered for an antitrust action because it controlled an overwhelming share of the market for sucker rods used in oil wells. The company's product was not unique, merely a threaded steel tube. What's more, several major steel companies also supplied the item.

The company's reply to the charge was that its customers actually weren't buying sucker rods at all. They were buying service. A shortage of the parts meant costly delays for well operators. So the supplier offered large stocks close to the fields. It even provided helicopter delivery when needed. This is what the customers saw as valuable and what they were willing to pay for.

Does the buyer of a watch purchase a time-keeping instrument, or a piece of jewelry? Does the purchaser of a bottle want a glass container, a reusable container, a convenient container, or an attractive container? You can see the competitive implications in each definition of the buyers' needs. Is a beer customer buying a beverage, or an image associated with a brand? Is the customer for solar heating equipment interested in the inherent value of solar, or does he simply want the cheapest long-term source of heat? Questions like these will help define your competitive choices.

Take the case of watches. A few years ago, the digital watch became a cheap and versatile competitor to the traditional mechanical watch. But manufacturers like Rolex did not jump onto the digital bandwagon. These companies knew that their customers really valued the status and decorative aspects of the product. Design appeal has helped their watches to hold market share.

Substitution

An immediate follow-up question is: Given the customer's needs and values, what are his choices? A purchaser of a saw is not buying a saw, he's buying a way of cutting. How else could he cut? With heat? With high pressure water? With a laser? What are the advantages and disadvantages of each method? Why does the customer choose the saw? Why might he choose another method tomorrow?

You are now considering the question of *substitution,* looking at function rather than at a particular product or service. This is a necessary preparation for competitive analysis because substitution can represent one of the most potent of all competitive threats. In the past 30 years, a maker of glass bottles would have seen a large part of his customer base desert him, first for steel and aluminum cans, then for plastic containers. If he'd concentrated his competitive view only on other bottlemakers, he would have been blind to the real threats.

Substitution has many competitive implications. When the home insulation market experienced a boom in demand during the energy crisis of the 1970s, makers of fiberglass insulation weren't in a position to drastically increase profit margins because of the possibility that home owners and builders would turn to substitutes like cellulose and styrofoam.

Many companies in the contract guard business, including firms like Burns International and Pinkerton, have had to face the threat that customers would turn to improved alarm systems and other security hardware as a substitute for guards. They have attempted to meet the challenge by getting into the alarm business themselves, as well as by offering consulting services and devising security systems incorporating both guards and hardware.

Every company should constantly look for potential substitutes. Could a rivet replace a screw? Could plastic replace steel? Soft drinks have proven to be a substitute for milk—and the dairy industry has suffered competitively. New technology can give rise to powerful substitutes. Electronic answering machines have cut into the market for traditional answering services. The mobile telephone now being popularized as a result of cellular systems could represent a blow to the two-way radio industry.

The availability of substitutes may force you to rethink the definition of your business. For example, a maker of copper cables may see that fiber optic devices are going to capture a portion of his market. He must decide whether he is in the cable business only, or whether he wants to be in the message transmission business. If the latter, he may be forced to begin developing fiber optics. If the former, he may have to specialize in a niche of the copper cable market that's not susceptible to substitution.

Analyzing Key Factors

The executives of a retail chain were convinced that the main competitive advantage they held was their highly efficient distribution system.

This was the focus of their competitive efforts. To make sure they were right, they hired a consulting firm to study their market. The findings: Distribution was not nearly as important a factor distinguishing one chain from another as they had thought.

The key to their success was really the talent and buying skill of individual branch managers. This is where they had the edge over competitors. The result: The chain's executives placed appropriate emphasis on recruiting the best store managers they could, and retaining the ones they had.

Can you accurately name the key competitive factors in your market *and* back up your judgment with facts? Too many managers immediately think of the obvious elements such as price, product quality, or brand recognition. These may indeed be key factors. But often more careful study will uncover different battlefields on which competitive struggles are taking place.

Consider two products and some of the competitive factors associated with each, listed in the following list from most to least important.

. . . .

1. Toothpaste

Distribution. If the product is not on the shelves of supermarkets and drugstores, it will not gain any significant market share.

Brand Recognition. The level and effectiveness of advertising is closely linked to market success.

Promotion. Coupons and in-store displays are an important competitive arena.

Price. Not as important a competitive factor. Price cutting can actually damage the product's image.

Product Characteristics. A few standard categories with only minor variations among brands. Unimportant.

Product Quality. No discernible differences. Not a factor.

2. Punch Press

Product Quality. Durability and efficiency are key factors in customers' buying choices.

> ***Service.*** The ability to quickly repair an out-of-service machine is critical to customers' needs.
>
> ***Product Characteristics.*** Improved controls, ease of setup, or enhanced safety features may be selling points.
>
> ***Price.*** A factor, but not the most important one.
>
> ***Brand Recognition.*** Purchase decisions are based on buyers' evaluations of a particular machine rather than on brand name.
>
> ***Distribution.*** Method of distribution or availability of product are not critical factors.
>
> . . . .

You can see that the key factors in one industry could be negligible in another. Always keep in mind that you are interested in *relative* importance. Distribution and brand-name recognition may be the main areas of struggle in toothpaste competition, but that doesn't mean that a company that produces an inferior or inconsistent product will still be able to compete. Competition in the beer industry is overwhelmingly based on the key factor of brand recognition and loyalty. But when Schlitz, a major American brewery, changed the formula of its product in 1974, the altered product proved to be unacceptable to many customers. This factor, while not traditionally a key one in the business, led to a serious decline in market share from which the company never recovered. The point is that key factors are not the only factors.

The Effects of Key Factors on Competition

The pharmaceutical industry provides a good example of the competitive implications that can arise from a single key factor. Product uniqueness has always been *the* factor on which competition in the drug industry has turned. Successful companies have had to produce a series of patented new products in order to maintain their high profit margins. But this factor has led to attacks on several fronts:

High profit margins have attracted chemical firms such as Dow

Chemical and consumer product firms such as Procter & Gamble, both of which entered the drug business in recent years.

Foreign companies have also been attracted to the U.S. market, with imports up 34 percent in 1984, capturing 10 percent of the market.

Aided by legislation, hospitals and consumers are turning increasingly to less expensive generic drugs.

The key factor has also determined the way that the industry has responded in defending itself against these challenges:

The companies have stepped up research and development. Merck & Co., for example, increased research and development spending to $400 million in 1984. They are building on their principal strengths.

They are concentrating resources. SmithKline recently sold $30 million in real estate interests plus a number of industrial operations in order to focus on pharmaceuticals.

Companies like Pfizer are staking out small positions in generic drug manufacture as a backup.

All these competitive moves, both offensive and defensive, are related to the single factor—proprietary products. In every industry, the best competitors are those companies that recognize which factors are most important and base their competitive strategies on them. Less successful firms often fail to look for the key factors, or concentrate on the wrong ones.

Key Product Factors

The automobile industry provides a lesson in the importance of key product-related factors. Product design was the key to competition in U.S. autos during the 1950s and 1960s. Not only did companies like General Motors, Ford, and Chrysler compete on the basis of radical yearly design changes, but the design factor discouraged new com-

Critical Parameters

For each key factor there are critical parameters that further define the competitive struggle. For example, speed of delivery is a key factor in the freight forwarding business. But if speed is charted against customer satisfaction, the increase in satisfaction for four-day delivery compared with five-day delivery will be minimal. But the satisfaction level for next-day delivery will be considerably higher than for two-day delivery.

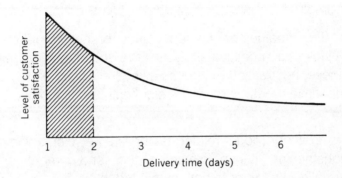

Participants in the freight forwarding business could therefore identify the two-day to overnight period as a critical parameter. Federal Express founder Fred Smith did just this, and revolutionized the industry by offering overnight delivery at a premium price. Less astute competitors were forced to follow suit after Federal Express was strongly established in the market.

Every key factor will have its critical parameters. Personal computer buyers may look on memory capacity as a key factor. But only within a certain range will added memory significantly increase competitive advantage. Beyond that range, the added capacity will be superfluous. National advertising will increase brand recognition for a consumer product. But after a certain saturation point, the increased exposure will produce only minimal competitive gains.

It's important not only to recognize key factors, but to know the parameters within which the greatest competitive advantage can be obtained.

petitors. Changeover costs were prohibitive for companies without the economies of scale of major U.S. firms, and foreign companies couldn't match the styling and color choices that U.S. makers offered to customers.

Focusing on design, U.S. executives ignored the fact that three other product factors—engineering, quality of construction, and gas mileage—would soon become the key to competition. In 1973, then-Ford executive Lee Iacocca said of U.S. auto buyers, "Give them leather— they can smell it." Styling, in other words, was everything.

But the U.S. companies paid a heavy price for their complacency and apparent lack of competitive analysis. Foreign companies, particularly the Japanese, neutralized design as a key factor and excelled in the new competitive areas, capturing a significant portion of the U.S. market.

Reliability, another product-related factor, is a key element in competition in industries as diverse as machine tools and computers. Consistency of quality is a factor in both semiconductor chips and textiles. Method of production can be a key factor, as when a company using robotics cuts labor costs or boosts consistency to attain a decided edge over a competitor using older methods.

Product uniqueness is often a key in competitive battles, as illustrated in pharmaceuticals. Procter & Gamble, by virtually inventing laundry detergent, was able to capture 70 percent of the U.S. market and still sells more than half of such products. Polaroid and Xerox both became major industrial companies by virtue of unique patented processes.

One competitive strategy is to create a product factor where none was previously important. For example, marketing factors had dominated the ice cream market until a small New York company produced its Häagen-Dazs brand—a denser and richer variety. This opened up a new arena of competition. Major manufacturers like Borden had to scramble to put new, competing products on the market rather than just step up promotion of their standard varieties.

Numerous other product-related factors can have an impact on competition: taste, purity, speed, ease of use, ease of maintenance, durability, versatility, weight, energy consumption, safety, or materials. What is important is to recognize those that are key in your industry today, and those that might become important tomorrow.

Marketing Factors

Price is an obvious marketing factor in competition. In commodity industries like chemicals, it may be virtually the sole area of rivalry. Many other factors, though, can have equal or greater influence on how firms compete.

Marketing factors tend to gain in importance when competing products have similar characteristics. Advertising and promotion are key competitive factors in selling consumer items such as soap, soft drinks, and cosmetics. An effective sales force may make the difference in office supplies, industrial maintenance products, or packaging materials.

Distribution can be a vital factor in marketing competition. When Beatrice Companies spent $2.8 billion to acquire Esmark, Inc., company executives admitted that one of the reasons for the move was to gain the advantages of the distribution system developed by Esmark's Hunt-Wesson division, considered to be the best in the industry. Since distribution is crucial in processed food competition, Beatrice hoped the tactic would help all its products gain on rivals in access to supermarkets.

Leasing rather than selling products may be a key competitive factor. Both Xerox and IBM used lease arrangements with customers to reach a broad market as well as to make market entry extremely expensive for competitors. Newcomers to the copier or computer fields had to invest large amounts of capital in leased products in order to match the terms of the market leaders.

Sometimes key marketing factors in an industry aren't very apparent. For example, credit terms can often be very important. The willingness of toy or apparel makers to extend generous credit terms to customers may be a critical competitive weapon. Auto companies like

General Motors and appliance makers like General Electric have developed their own credit subsidiaries to provide financing to buyers. In times of high interest rates, the cost of that financing can be a key factor in winning customers.

Environmental Factors

Not all competitive factors arise directly from products or marketing. Some have their origins in the outside world. Dealing with government regulation, for example, can be an element of competition. Part of AT&T's traditional strategy for remaining competitive was to head off government regulation through efficient service and skillful public relations. The deregulation of the airline industry led to a drastically changed competitive climate and helped new entrants like People Express to gain market share.

Demographics often represent an environmental factor with a big influence on competition. Saks Fifth Avenue realized that the rise in number of working women meant that many potential customers no longer had the leisure time to shop. The store instituted a shopping service to help customers spend their time—and money—more efficiently. Other firms have been fashioning competitive strategies intended to capture the patronage of the growing percentage in the population of older people.

Trends can be a crucial and volatile competitive factor. Increasing the awareness of the role of nutrition in health has helped companies with "natural" products capture share from other competitors. Yogurt makers, for example, have gained at the expense of other foods. Apparel, shoe, and sporting goods companies are competing for the market generated by the fitness boom.

A variety of environmental factors have transformed competition in the tobacco industry. Findings on the negative effects of smoking combined with government regulations and changing tastes turned low-tar cigarettes into a growth market, with competitive struggles developing between brands like Philip Morris' Merit and R.J. Reynolds' Vantage.

Slow growth in cigarette sales sent the companies looking for niches where the market was expanding such as in premium cigarettes (Philip Morris' Players) and in generic brands (pioneered by the Liggett Group).

Yet another competitive development has been the fact that tobacco companies have shifted assets and competitive attention away from cigarettes—R.J. Reynolds moving into restaurants, liquor, and food processing; Philip Morris, into beer and soft drinks.

Sizing Up Your Business

Competitive Analysis Worksheet 2 will help you develop a structured evaluation of your business, your customers, and the key factors in your market. Reproduce it and fill it out for each distinct product line or market segment in which you operate. For example, if you produce both custom and commodity items, the customer needs and key factors are likely to be different in each case.

As you develop your competitive anlaysis program, let your answers to these questions guide your priorities. For example, your analysis of key factors will point to areas where you should maintain a close watch on competitors, and other areas that are relatively insignificant. And considering possible substitutes should give you an idea of important areas outside your immediate industry that you will have to track.

COMPETITIVE ANALYSIS WORKSHEET 2

BUSINESS DEFINITION AND KEY COMPETITIVE FACTORS

Completed by _____ Date _____

Product/division _____

1. What business is your company/division in?

   _____

2. What aspects about your company/division are unique?

   _____

   _____

3. Have you defined a corporate mission?   ___ Yes   ___ No

   What is it? _____

   _____

4. How would you define your market niche?

   _____

   _____

5. Has your company's business or niche changed in the past five years?

   ___ Yes   ___ No

   How? _____

   _____

6. Do you expect it to change in the next five years?

   ___ Yes   ___ No

   How? _____

   _____

7. Who are your company's primary customers?

_____

_____

8. What do your customers consider most valuable in your products (e.g., service, durability, precision, etc.)?

_____

_____

9. Which group of your customers is most satisfied with your products and why?

_____

_____

10. Which group is least satisfied and why?

_____

_____

11. Which group of potential customers is your major competitor selling to that your company/division isn't?

_____

Why haven't you entered that portion of the market?

_____

_____

12. Which group of customers do you sell to that your major competitor doesn't?

_____

Why have you been successful in this market area?

_____

_____

13. Have the needs of your customers changed in any way in the past five years?

_____ Yes _____ No

In what direction?

_____

_____

14. Are your customers' needs likely to change over the next five years?

_____ Yes _____ No

In what direction?

_____

_____

15. What function does your product serve for your customers?

_____

_____

16. List three potential substitutes for your product.

a. _____

b. _____

c. _____

17. What are the most important reasons that your customers use your product instead of these substitutes (e.g., lower cost, greater reliability, etc.)?

a. _____

b. _____

c. _____

18. How could each of the substitutes be made more feasible so as to be a competitive threat to you?

a. _____

b. _____

c. _____

19. List the two most important competitive factors in each of the following areas of your industry (if applicable).

   a. Product related _____

   _____

   b. Marketing related _____

   _____

   c. Environmental _____

   _____

20. Of the factors listed, which one is the most decisive today in competition in your industry?

   _____

21. What are the critical parameters of this factor (e.g., crucial quality level, speed of service, area of price resistance, etc.)?

   _____

   _____

22. How has your company tried to gain the competitive edge in this area?

   _____

   _____

23. How have major rivals tried to gain the competitive edge in the same area?

   _____

   _____

24. In what ways are you vulnerable to competition in this area?

   _____

   _____

4

Laying the Foundation for a Competitive Analysis System

In 1973, Jerry L. Wall, management professor at Western Illinois University, polled 1,200 managers, asking: "Do you think your company should have a more systematic method of gathering, analyzing, and reporting information about competitors?" As reported in the *Harvard Business Review,* 72 percent of the respondents, representing many different companies and industries, answered in the affirmative.

Since then, more and more companies have come to realize that this crucial function cannot be handled simply "as needed." It cannot be left to chance. Among the ranks of companies that now systematically keep track of competitors are consumer products firms like Eastman Kodak and General Mills, industrial companies such as Boeing and Monsanto, and international firms like Hoffman-LaRoche and Mitsubishi Heavy Industries.

Naturally, companies are reluctant to disclose specific details of their competitor analysis efforts. They don't want to tip their hands to the very competitors they're tracking. But the Alexander Hamilton Institute has done its own survey with industry insiders to produce the general advice and five-step program that follows.

Shaping the Structure to Your Company

Competitive analysis systems vary widely in structure because the requirements for competitor information are so diverse. In some circumstances, competitor analysis may be handled primarily by one manager, with information stored in a few file drawers. On the other hand, a major telecommunications firm recently spent $500,000 to set up a computerized information-processing system devoted to competitor analysis, and budgeted $150,000 annually to run the program.

One thing you definitely want to avoid is adding unnecessarily to your company's bureaucracy or paperwork. A "lean" organization will always give you the best results in competitor analysis. The scope of your effort, though, is not necessarily dependent on the size of your company. A 10-person electronics firm whose products are on the cutting edge of technology may need a highly organized effort with in-depth capabilities in order to keep up with competitive developments.

A national mining company may need only the simplest competitor analysis system.

Here are the factors you should consider to determine the scope of your own efforts:

Your company's competitive stance (expansion plans, effort to increase market share, etc.)

The volatility of your markets

The intensity of competition in your markets

The complexity of your market, your customers' needs, and so forth

The rate of change in your industry (in technology, marketing techniques, etc.)

The diversity of your operations (e.g., international scope)

The information needs of your strategic planning group

Figure 1 offers a schematic representation of the role of competitor analysis in a company. Think about the ways in which it applies to your firm.

Setting Up the Program

Almost every company already engages in some competitor analysis. Your answers in Competitive Analysis Worksheet 1 have given you an idea of the current scope of your efforts. Just as you have to shape your competitive analysis program to the specific needs of your company, you also want to modify it to incorporate the techniques and procedures you are already using. Keep both of these goals in mind as you implement the following five steps.

Step 1: Clarify the Goals

You've already examined the reasons you need a competitive analysis program. Now you have to establish specific goals for your effort.

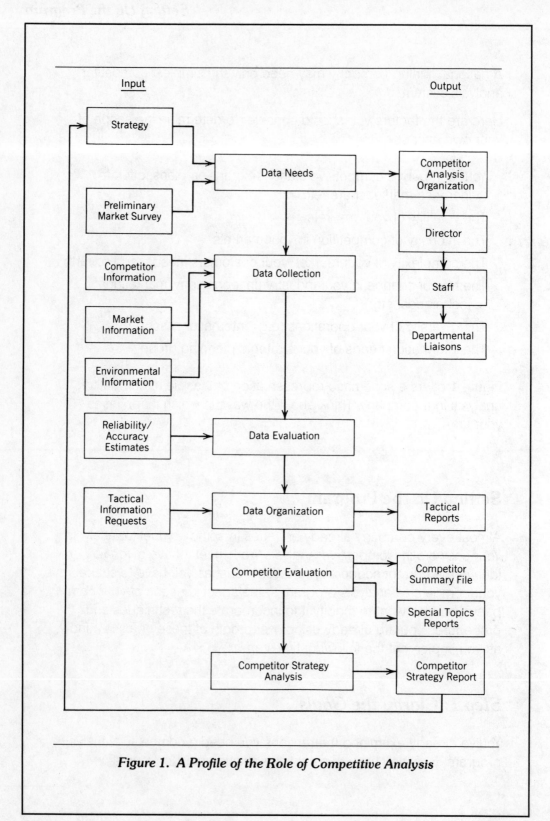

Input   Output

Strategy

Preliminary Market Survey

Data Needs

Competitor Analysis Organization

Director

Competitor Information

Market Information

Data Collection

Staff

Departmental Liaisons

Environmental Information

Reliability/ Accuracy Estimates

Data Evaluation

Tactical Information Requests

Data Organization

Tactical Reports

Competitor Evaluation

Competitor Summary File

Special Topics Reports

Competitor Strategy Analysis

Competitor Strategy Report

Figure 1. A Profile of the Role of Competitive Analysis

For example, one industrial products distributor decided that the sources of information about competitors that it had been relying on—sales staff reports and trade journals—were those that were most convenient. The first priority of the competitive analysis director was to develop a much wider range of sources so as to compile a more thorough picture of the competitive landscape.

Another firm felt that its vice-president of planning was doing a good job of analysis, but that competitor information and evaluation was not reaching the line managers who needed it for day-to-day decisions. This company established wider dissemination as its primary goal.

Most companies will choose several important goals for their competitive analysis effort. By setting these priorities, you can better tailor the structure of your program to your specific needs. The following list contains some actual goals that companies we surveyed have established. Think over each one and decide how it would rank in your firm. Keep them in mind when you fill out Section A in Analysis Worksheet 3 at the end of this chapter.

Competitor Analysis Goals

To accumulate greater depth of competitor information

To keep data files more current

To select pertinent information, reduce information overload

To channel information to decision makers

To consolidate data from various internal sources

To review a wider range of sources

To analyze and draw conclusions from information

To ask the right questions about company strategy

To help line managers understand the sources of competitive advantage

To help plan for contingencies

To formulate competitive strategies and tactics

To monitor long-term and environmental trends

To track short-term developments more closely

To disseminate and communicate competitor information

· ·

Information Key

Answer the following two questions to give yourself a quick focus on what competitor analysis means to your company. This may point you toward the most important goals of your program.

1. Which piece of information that you've gained in the past about a competitor was the most useful in formulating actual strategic or tactical decisions? Why? Can you expand the scope of your investigation in the area from which that piece of information came?

_____

_____

_____

2. What information would you most like to have today about your principal competitor? What would you least like your competitor to get about you? What would be the sources?

_____

_____

_____

· ·

Step 2: Establish Responsibility

No matter what the size of the company or the scope of its competitor analysis program, nearly every company that has such a systematic effort assigns overall responsibility for competitor analysis to one person. He may have a group of assistants or work alone. Competitor analysis may be his sole duty or he may only spend part of his time on it. But it is crucial that someone should direct and be answerable for the effort.

There are three very clear reasons for this:

Well-defined responsibility prevents overlap and wasted effort.

Competitor analysis must draw on all areas of the organization, and without a central authority this consolidation won't work.

If no one is answerable for competitive analysis, the task is likely to be assigned a low priority or never be accomplished at all.

Here are the qualifications experts recommend for a successful competitive analysis director.

High enough in the organization so that he can interact with top-level planners and decision makers. Many companies give the duty to a vice-president of marketing or finance, others to someone from the planning department. What's important is not to assign the duty to a clerk or a first-level manager.

Should have wide operating experience. Competitive analysis directors have to know what is important so that they can successfully filter and analyze information. Should be familiar with procedures and terminology in marketing, manufacturing, and product development.

Skills should include an ability to work with people, since interaction with managers from all areas of the company is a requirement.

Should be analytical and thorough, but creativity and imagination are more important than a knack for detail.

While the director may be a specialist (e.g., in marketing or engineering), he should not be narrow-minded but should recognize the different needs of all facets of the company.

. . . .

Information Key

Further focus your sights on a good candidate to assume competitor analysis duties by answering the following questions:

1. Who fits the above list of qualifications most closely?

_____

2. Which manager has shown the most interest in competitor topics?

_____

3. Who has been most involved in competitor analysis in the past?

_____

. . . .

Figure 2 gives a composite job description for a director of competitive analysis assembled from the files of actual companies. Modify it to fit the specific needs of your firm. Then use it to help guide your selection of an executive to fill this role and to aid him in defining his duties.

The director of competitive analysis typically reports to the vice-president of marketing. A senior officer responsible for planning would also be a logical person for the director to report to. In smaller companies, the competitive analysis director may even report directly to the chief executive. What's important is that the director have quick and easy access to top management.

Step 3: Decide on the Staff

The number of people working directly under the competitive analysis director depends on the scope of your program. The best procedure is to start with the smallest feasible group and to add people only as needed. A few experienced staff members are always preferable to a larger number of low-level employees. For example, a trained engineer will be immensely more valuable as a researcher than a clerk. The former will be able to identify valuable information, while the latter may accumulate data indiscriminately.

Not all the competitive analysis staff members have to be assigned on a full-time basis. Section B of Competitive Analysis Worksheet 3 lets you fill in the initial assistants who will work directly under the competitive analysis director.

Step 4: Establish Departmental Liaisons

This is a vital aspect of making competitor analysis work. It connects the function directly with those who will be using the information and evaluation generated so the process doesn't turn into a mere formality.

Departmental liaisons are individuals within each department who work with the competitive analysis director while continuing to work for

POSITION DESCRIPTION

Director of Competitive Analysis

Reports to   Vice-President, Marketing

Supervises   Assigned staff
                         Departmental liaisons

Basic Function

   The director of competitive analysis is responsible for collecting, compiling, and analyzing all pertinent information on the activities, resources, and plans of current or potential competitor companies. He is also responsible for identifying the key factors in the company's competitive environment and bringing any significant changes in these factors to the attention of appropriate managers.

Primary Duties and Responsibilities

   1. Develops and implements plans and objectives for his staff.
   2. Devises a system for the efficient and thorough collection of important competitor information, including:
      a. An in-house audit of possible information sources
      b. A means of reviewing all relevant publications on a timely basis
      c. A means of tapping third-party and governmental sources in a systematic way
   3. Establishes a system for filtering information to select relevant data and for filing such data in an orderly and accessible manner for the use of all concerned managers.
   4. Sets up and maintains a data base on each significant competitor firm and on any specific market or industry matters deemed relevant.
   5. Oversees and directs the activities of ad hoc committees composed of managers from various disciplines with the purpose of:
      a. Conducting an in-depth study of a competitor's strategic plans
      b. Reviewing contingencies
      c. Studying possible competitor reaction to company activities
      d. Conducting any other special studies deemed necessary

Figure 2. A Composite Description for a Competitive Analysis Program Director

6. Supplies appropriate tactical competitor information and estimates as requested.

7. Counsels with appropriate managers in marketing, planning, or other areas in relation to competitor activities, resources, or plans and their current or future impact on the company.

8. Develops and recommends the organizational structure, staffing, compensation, hiring, termination, transfer, and promotion of all personnel under his direct supervision.

Principal Working Relationships
(excluding direct reporting relationships)

1. Works with managers and committees in the area of strategic planning in order to ensure proper consideration of competitive factors in the formulation of plans.

2. Works with individual department heads in order to facilitate the efficient transfer of all relevant data to the competitive analysis group, to respond to information needs of specific departments, and to assure the dissemination of relevant competitor evaluations to the departments affected.

3. Transmits periodic reports to the chief executive officer and other designated members of top management highlighting important competitor developments and contingencies and recommending possible responses.

Figure 2. (*continued*)

their specific department head. A manager just below the level of department head—assistant sales manager, for example—is usually the best person for this role. The departmental liaisons should be drawn from various areas, including purchasing, engineering, marketing, finance, and personnel. After consulting with department heads and the competitive analysis director, fill in the names of these liaisons in Section C of Analysis Worksheet 3.

Step 5: Plan Ad Hoc Committees

The purpose of the standing competitive analysis group is to maintain a data base on competitors and market conditions, to track key competitive factors, and to contribute assessments and information to the

. . . .

The duties of each liaison, as assigned by the competitive analysis director, will be:

1. To oversee the collection of data from his department and its flow to the competitive analysis group.
2. To analyze and disseminate competitive information that is of specific interest to his department.
3. To communicate to the competitive analysis director the information needs of his department and to make sure key areas are being tracked.
4. To maintain and develop information sources within, or related to, his department.
5. To contribute expertise in the department's function to ad hoc committees, contingency planning, and so forth.

. . . .

planning process, as well as to carry out routine data-collection, assessment, and dissemination duties. For many other goals, though, the competitive analysis director should draw together ad hoc groups, both because the projects are temporary and because they require a wider range of expertise. The groups may be composed of departmental liaisons or other senior department managers. They should be led by a group leader who reports to the competitive analysis director and convened after a well-defined goal and subgoals are drawn up.

The makeup of the committees must reflect the specific task. For example, a group assigned to analyze competitive response to a new product might include managers from marketing, sales, engineering and finance. One concerned with a competitor's cost and pricing would include financial analysts, production managers, and sales reps.

Some of the purposes for which companies have assembled these ad hoc committees include:

To make an initial in-depth study of a competitor

To evaluate potential competitor reactions to a major market move, such as a new product introduction, a change in pricing strategy, and so forth

To study market configuration (growth, capacity, etc.) before a capital project such as a plant expansion

To study significant competitor actions (a merger, a new advertising campaign, etc.)

To conduct a country study before entering a foreign market or when such markets become volatile

Competitive Analysis Procedures

Competitive Analysis Worksheet 3 lists in Section D a number of specific responsibilities that the director must undertake or assign to subordinates. Once your competitive analysis program has been established, go through these items and make sure all have been covered.

1. Define the Issues. The competitive analysis director should continually review and communicate to top management the key factors in competition. These can change overnight. Iowa Beef Processors, for example, threw the meat industry into turmoil when it began shipping packaged rather than bulk beef. Competitors had to scramble to deal with this new competitive factor. Many lost market share in the process.

Other important issues include who the company should regard as competitors, which firms may become competitors in the future, how the firm is vulnerable to competitors' tactics, and where opportunities might arise to improve the company's position in relation to competitors.

2. Maintain the Data Base. Information ages quickly. Yesterday's data may not apply to today's realities. The competitive analysis director must adopt procedures that assure that decision makers are receiving the most current facts. Some ways to keep files up-to-date include:

Semiannual strategic reviews of key competitors by ad hoc committees

· ·

Information Key

1. Imagine you are calling together an ad hoc analysis committee to study a competitor tactic, such as a significant price drop. What would you assign as the principal goals of such a task force?

_____

_____

_____

2. Who would be the logical managers to comprise such a group?

_____

_____

_____

· ·

An annual review of all competitors, with monthly tracking of key factors

Analytic reviews by ad hoc committees triggered by predetermined events (e.g., a competitor gains more than two percent in market share)

These techniques should be adopted in addition to filing and analysis of all incoming competitor information. Their purpose is to turn information into a basis for action or reaction in relation to the overall competitive climate.

3. Determine Consistency. A company is acting consistently if its actions are in accord with both its goals and its environment. That means a firm that wants to gain market share in a price-sensitive market is acting consistently if it lowers prices. If the firm takes the same approach to a market that is segmented according to product features and quality and isn't price-sensitive, then its action is inconsistent.

Inconsistency often represents a weakness in a competitor's strategy that can be exploited by your firm. An example of consistency is Texas Instruments' strategy of being a price leader in integrated circuits. The company had the technical and production expertise to do so, and was able to generate the volume that made the goal achievable. On the other hand, Clark Equipment has tried to maintain a position as a full-line manufacturer of industrial equipment, but has neither the price advantage nor the technical lead to do so. This inconsistency has allowed Clark's competitors to make inroads into its market.

4. Spread Competitor Awareness. The director should adopt procedures that make every employee aware of the importance of keeping an eye on competitors. Meetings run by departmental liaisons, updates on company performance relative to key competitors, or bonus systems geared to industry or competitor averages are a few ways of doing this.

Pitfalls to Avoid

Among the companies in our competitive analysis survey, these were the most common mistakes and difficulties encountered when setting up an analysis program.

1. Overload. This occurs when you gather so much information that relevant data becomes lost among trivia. Set goals and focus your competitor analysis on key factors. Don't assume that the best system is the one that gathers the most information. Be selective.

2. The Library. Some companies drifted into a tendency to gather archives for history. What you want is data that can influence actions today. While it can be useful to track trends, most data that is simply collected and filed away turns stale and useless. Your job is to analyze, not to act as librarian. Don't document the past; prepare for the future.

3. Too General. The number of consumers in West Germany who use upright versus tank-type vacuum cleaners is a specific fact that might be useful to an appliance maker who is considering competing in the German market. The total industrial output in West Germany last year

. . . .

Information Key

Focus on the level of competitor awareness that currently exists in your company by asking:

1. How aware are managers of who your main competitors are?

_____

_____

_____

2. How can you get managers to compare their performances to those of a competitor rather than to an in-house standard?

_____

_____

3. Does a sense of rivalry exist among employees in relation to specific competitors?

_____

_____

_____

. . . .

is a general piece of data with little direct relevance. Your main competitor's total research spending is general; his spending on upgrading product X is specific—and perhaps vital. Always try to determine and search out the information that will have an impact on your own plans and strategies. Don't get lost in research for its own sake.

4. Limited Focus. Some companies concentrate their whole competitor analysis effort on one major rival. They see themselves in head-to-head competition with this firm, ignoring diverse threats from other competitors and substitutes.

. . . .

Action Probes

You are now on your way to creating an organized competitive anlaysis effort. Begin thinking about ways this system will help you with business decisions by asking:

What plans do you currently have on the drawing board that will benefit from increased competitor information?

Where do you suspect weaknesses or inconsistencies might exist in the strategies of your competitors?

What facet of his business do you think your principal competitor would *least* like you to know about? Why?

. . . .

Other companies look only at one aspect of competition, such as price. This can undermine your competitive response. For example, your competitors may be offering comparable products at the same price you do, but still be luring your customers with advantageous credit terms, improved product specifications, or a longer warranty.

5. Obsession with Numbers. Don't waste time trying to estimate your competitors' sales to the penny, his capacity to the last piece. Don't focus exclusively on quantity and ignore qualitative factors. The most useful competitor data is often "soft"—rumors that turn out to be true; rough estimates that indicate major developments; trends and strategies.

COMPETITIVE ANALYSIS WORKSHEET 3

COMPETITOR ANALYSIS GROUP: ACTION PLAN

Director _____

Reports to _____

Additional (or principal) duties _____

Section A: Goals

In order of priority, list the three most important initial goals of your competitive analysis group:

1. _____

2. _____

3. _____

Section B: Staff

List the initial members of the competitive analysis group staff, their main functions, to whom they report, and whether they are assigned to the group on a full-time or part-time basis:

Member	Function	Reports to	FT/PT

Section C: Departmental Liaisons

List all the departmental liaisons and the departments from which they will report:

Liaison	Dept.	Liaison	Dept.
_____	_____	_____	_____
_____	_____	_____	_____
_____	_____	_____	_____
_____	_____	_____	_____

Section D: Assignment Checklist

Responsibility	Assigned to	Urgency (High/Med./ Low)	Completion Date/ Ongoing
Establish competitive analysis group structure	_____	_____	_____
Set up basic procedures	_____	_____	_____
Identify in-house information sources	_____	_____	_____
Conduct in-house information audit	_____	_____	_____
Identify and develop third-party sources	_____	_____	_____
Organize published sources	_____	_____	_____
Stimulate competitive awareness inside company	_____	_____	_____
Set up competitor data bases	_____	_____	_____
Coordinate departmental liaisons	_____	_____	_____
Establish filing system	_____	_____	_____
Systematically weed files	_____	_____	_____

Responsibility	Assigned to	Urgency (High/Med./ Low)	Completion Date/ Ongoing
Organize file update procedure	_____	_____	_____
Set trigger events for strategic review	_____	_____	_____
Establish channels to disseminate information	_____	_____	_____
Arrange input into planning process	_____	_____	_____

5

Developing Research Techniques and In-House Information Sources

The most common problem encountered when collecting information on competitors is not a lack but an overabundance of data. Selectivity, recognition of which sources provide the most *useful* information for your company, and an awareness of the depth of research needed should be the guiding principles for the competitive analysis program. You want quality, not quantity. Constant evaluation and scrutiny will avoid information overload.

Research Techniques

Good competitor research is an art as much as a science. Experience is the most valuable guide to quick and efficient compilation of quality data. The following guidelines will help to get your research off to a fast start. Begin by setting goals.

What do we need to know?

Which competitors do we need to investigate?

These two questions define the scope of your data collection. Direct competitors who are operating in your geographic area and are expanding market share at your expense clearly demand extensive research. You want to know as much about them as possible—their marketing techniques, products, financial resources, management philosophy, relations with customers and suppliers, and so forth.

In the case of potential competitors who haven't yet introduced directly competing products into your market, you need only general facts—business priorities, research in critical areas, overall market strategies. For companies between these two extremes—firms in your industry who are not now selling their products in your geographic area, for example—you have to determine an appropriate research goal.

The important thing is to clarify all those goals. Rank research needs according to competitive priorities. Don't try to track 50 different competitors in depth. Do a thorough analysis of your three or four most

. . . .

Information Key

To start thinking about these goals, list three competitors: a direct rival, an indirect rival, and a potential rival. Briefly sketch out the depth of information you need about each.

Competitor 1: _____

_____

_____

Competitor 2: _____

_____

_____

Competitor 3: _____

_____

_____

. . . .

important rivals. Don't try to gain detailed knowledge of every aspect of every competitor's business. But keep up-to-date on key competitive factors.

Assembling the Pieces

Don't expect to gain a thorough view of a competitive company all at once. Research always involves gathering many bits of information—some of them seemingly insignificant. As you build up data and assemble a picture, new bits of data will become increasingly revealing.

For example, a marketing planner at a plastics company uncovered information about a competitor's polyethylene film division. The facts included:

The hiring of two new salespeople

A rumored contract with an additional supplier of feedstocks

A $3 million line of credit negotiated with a local bank

A building permit for a warehouse

While none of these pieces of information alone would have told the story, together they indicated that the division was planning a significant increase in volume of production. Would the competitor try to gain volume by lowering prices? By expanding its market coverage? By entering a new segment? The planner decided his own company had better start preparing for these contingencies.

Don't Ignore the Obvious

Don't make information gathering more difficult or more expensive than necessary. You may have to check many sources to find out one fact. But other times you can find the information you're seeking in the most obvious places, as the following executives did.

A manager at a welding company wanted to find out if a competitor had expanded its work force. To do so, he simply called the firm's personnel manager and asked. The personnel manager told him that they not only weren't hiring, they'd just laid off 10 laborers.

A legal services firm was interested in the market coverage of a competitor. After considering hiring a market research firm, the competitive analysis director instead searched through regional phone book yellow pages. The listings told him where the rival was currently operating and which markets it hadn't yet entered.

Managers of a housewares manufacturer found that they could obtain better country studies for their international expansion by assigning the job to one of their own employees who was from the target country than they could by commissioning a consulting firm.

· ·

Information Key

1. List three easy and direct sources of competitor information that you've used in the past:

   _____

   _____

   _____

   _____

2. List three obvious sources for information you might need in the future:

   _____

   _____

   _____

   _____

· ·

Go into the Field

While much information can be obtained from published sources, field interviews are an essential part of all competitor research. Field sources have the advantage of being timely and pertinent. Their drawback is that the information they give can be subjective and hard to quantify. You can overcome these shortcomings by pressing for more detail and by seeking further sources to corroborate facts.

While it is useful to gather basic information from published sources before conducting the interview, don't try to cover all the literature first. Field contacts can usually direct you to more useful written sources, as well as to additional field sources.

The phone is a valuable tool in searching for particular bits of data, but a face-to-face interview often yields a great deal more information.

The field interview plays a role in many aspects of your research effort:

> Researchers can talk to a wide range of subjects, from competitors' suppliers to security analysts.
>
> Salespeople should know how to obtain useful information from customers.
>
> Engineers should be talking to colleagues from competing and related firms at conventions and seminars.

Figure 3 contains guidelines for gathering useful information through interviews. Duplicate it and distribute it to all those in the company who will be collecting information in the field. Ask them to review it frequently. Emphasize that it applies to both formal interviews and informal talks.

Reviewing Ethics

Two dangers exist in connection with the ethics of competitor research. Certain researchers—both competitor analysis staff members and other in-house information gatherers—may be tempted to engage in some form of espionage. Perhaps they think that spying and stealing are the best ways to obtain useful data. This is decidedly not the case. In fact, most valuable competitive data is available from completely legitimate sources. An intelligence analyst estimates that even the U.S. Navy obtains 95 percent of its peacetime intelligence from public sources. Industrial espionage does exist, but it is in no way vital or necessary to an effective competitor analysis program.

The second danger is that an unwillingness to create the appearance of espionage will keep your company from pursuing legal and ethical sources of data. Competitive research and analysis is both fair and necessary. A competitor may be disturbed, for example, that his distributor gives you information on his buying practices. But your requesting such information is in no way unethical. Don't let this fear hamper your competitor analysis effort.

GUIDELINES FOR CONDUCTING FIELD INTERVIEWS

1. Interview in person when possible. Set up the interview in advance. Be persistent in seeking interviews.

2. Prepare thoroughly. Plan questions, but be ready to improvise in order to pursue important points.

3. Always be honest about your company affiliation and, if asked, about the reason you are seeking the information.

4. Be observant. Important details can include: interviewee's emphasis or attitude, reluctance to talk about subjects, office or reading material, schedule, other visitors.

5. Normally, limit interviews to 45 minutes. Begin by building rapport, then ask important questions. Avoid digressions. Coax the subject back to pertinent topics. Keep the tone informal.

6. If appropriate, take detailed notes. Ask the subject for written documents to back up points made. Write a summary of the interview immediately afterward. Note subject's biases, reliability, and usefulness as a source.

7. Take a positive attitude. Assume the subject is willing to cooperate even if you can see no clear benefit to him. Many people enjoy demonstrating their expertise.

8. Ask for sensitive information indirectly. For example, a subject may be reluctant to discuss a competitor's sales in monetary terms, but may be willing to estimate the total market and the competitor's share of it.

9. Don't press the subject for exact numbers, but always urge him to give estimates or guesses.

10. Lead from industry-general topics to competitor-specific ones. Use leading questions when necessary. For example, if the subject is reluctant to estimate competitor's capital spending, ask, "Would you agree it's in the $8 to 9 million range?"

11. Be willing to trade information. Demonstrating your knowledge of the topic encourages the subject to talk and leaves him feeling that he's gained something from the interview.

12. Ask the subject to recommend other sources of information he thinks would be helpful.

Figure 3. Specific Steps for Collecting Field Information

The best way to handle this issue is for the competitive analysis director to review with all persons involved the guidelines of ethical behavior in this area. In most cases they parallel general business ethics—bribery, theft, or overt misrepresentation are wrong. Deliberate attempts to obtain trade secrets are unethical and may be illegal.

One rule of thumb that experienced researchers give: Ask yourself whether you'd be content to have the fact that you are using the contemplated information-gathering technique published on the front page of the newspaper. If you'd be embarrassed, don't do it.

How to Tap In-House Sources of Information

Your first priority in conducting any competitor research should be to make full use of all information sources within your own company. A thorough, well-organized network that gathers information from all departments will be the foundation of your competitive analysis effort.

During World War II, a U.S. infantryman was wounded while fighting on the island of Attu. When he was brought back to a field hospital, it was discovered that he'd picked up some Japanese papers as souvenirs. Intelligence officers found that the documents gave detailed information about enemy strongpoints on the island. The soldier could have avoided many days of battle—and his own injuries—if he'd turned over the information to his superiors at once.

Your "troops" in the war for market share can benefit from this example. Military theory holds that the best intelligence comes from small group commanders—in business that means from first-level managers and their subordinates. It is the salesperson, the purchasing agent, the product engineer who is likely to first know the "enemy's" moves. Make sure that all employees understand the value of looking for and passing on information about competitors. Emphasize that they should leave the task of deciding whether the data is important to competitive analysis experts.

The In-House Audit

You can reproduce Competitive Analysis Worksheet 4, found at the end of this chapter, and use it to structure your own internal audit. Its purpose is not to gather information directly, but to locate good sources of competitor data and to emphasize to departmental people the need to channel such information to the competitor analysis group. Note that the survey begins with questions about the department's own information needs, making clear that competitive analysis is a function that can help everyone in the company.

When the initial forms have been completed, the competitive analysis director should follow up by interviewing knowledgeable sources within the departments. This will not only help begin building the competitor information data base, but will also provide a clear idea of where to go for future information in specific areas.

For example, the director might want to debrief all employees who have worked for competitor firms. Instead of asking for trade secrets, he should focus on the structure and procedures of the competitor's management, its methods of doing business, company philosophy, compensation practices, the personalities of key managers, and similar topics.

The in-house audit should not be a one-time event. Leonard M. Fuld, president of Information Data Search, offers this advice based on his company's experience in helping clients conduct such audits: "The audit should become a system, not a single process. The effort needs to be refreshed periodically. It should combine forms, interviews, and data collection."

Overcoming Resistance

Don't be surprised if line managers and employees resist cooperating with competitor information gathering at first. For many managers, competitive analysis represents a threat. If the information gathered indicates relative competitor strengths—in sales results, productivity, hiring, advertising effectiveness, or any other area—then the manager feels that his performance suffers by comparison. He can no longer blame a market slump for slow sales growth if competitors' revenues are rising. He can't blame inflation for higher costs if competitors' costs haven't risen.

The way to overcome this resistance is to:

Emphasize that the information gathered will be used to help managers do their jobs better.

Talk in terms of solutions rather than scolding individual managers for not keeping up with competitors.

Set up a reward system based on improved performance relative to competitors or industry averages.

Specify that competitor information gathering is an integral part of every manager's job.

Departmental Contributions

Once the in-house audit is complete, the competitive analysis director and his staff can begin collecting data from in-house sources. Besides conducting interviews, they can request written information reports using the Competitive Information Reporting Form in Chapter 8. Some departments will also be able to forward documents and statistical reports kept within the department that can contribute to the central competitive analysis effort. Following are some examples of the type of data that might be available from selected departments.

Sales

Your company's salespeople are often the first to spot competitors' new products, changes in specifications, new selling tactics, price changes, or entry into new markets. They can also provide information on market conditions, customer needs, potential substitute products, trends, opportunities, and competitor weaknesses.

Here are some competitor questions that your sales force may be able to answer:

Why are customers switching to competitors' products?

Are competitors delivering orders on time?

What credit terms do competitors offer customers?

What complaints do customers have about competitors' products?

Are a competitor's sales increasing or decreasing?

Have new competitors entered the market?

What are competitors' sales strategies?

Do competing salespeople sell aggressively, or only take orders?

Engineering

Engineers, scientists, and technicians often have contacts with colleagues in their fields. These include not only their counterparts in competitor companies, but individuals in universities and government agencies who may be excellent sources of information on markets and trends.

For example, a precision instrument manufacturer hired a scientist who was an expert in filter technology. The hiring preceded a move into a new product area—advanced filtration devices. An engineer in a competing company heard about the hiring when it happened, knew the man's reputation and expertise, and alerted his own company's planners to the expected development.

Some companies are even more aggressive in using engineers to gather competitive data. For example, Intel Corp. offered to provide engineering help for certain key customers. These employees, working inside customers' plants, picked up information on the design and introduction schedule of a new semiconductor chip being developed by rival Motorola. Intel used the information to rush its own product to market and to urge large-volume users to design the Intel chip into

. . . .

Information Key

Contact the salesperson in your company with the most direct contact with your main competitor (e.g., serves the same customers). Formulate three specific questions about the competitor that you think he might be able to answer and see if he has the information or can get it:

1. _____

2. _____

3. _____

. . . .

their products. The result: Intel had grabbed a large share of the market before Motorola's new product was introduced.

Purchasing Agents

These are valuable and often overlooked sources of competitor data. Their contacts with suppliers can often provide early warnings of competitor moves. Try to find out from them:

Are competitors buying any materials or equipment out of the ordinary?

Which competitors are stockpiling materials? Why?

What changes are taking place in competitors' make/buy strategies?

What new materials are being used in the industry? Do they provide a cost advantage?

Which materials that a competitor uses are in short supply?

How will changing prices (of fuel, raw materials, components, etc.) affect specific competitors?

Personnel

Your personnel department should always be on the lookout for potential sources of competitor information. The personnel manager can

. . . .

Action Probes

Could your engineering department contribute more to strategic planning by evaluating competitors' technical directions?

Can you gain enough technical information on competitors' future products to design competitive advantages into your own?

How can you exploit specific technical weaknesses of particular competitors?

. . . .

identify employees who have worked for competitors or in key related firms. He should be alert to extract information from job applicants who have knowledge of a competitor's operations, even if they are not hired by your company. One company found that certain employees recruited from colleges had gained significant information on competitors through summer intern jobs.

During a job interview, candidates are often eager to talk about their role in their former company. A candidate at a computer peripherals company revealed the results of a software evaluation study conducted by his former employer.

Other Departments

Employees in manufacturing, accounting, legal, public relations, service, marketing, and other departments should not be ignored. In each area there will be individuals who can provide important competitive information—through personal contacts, trade sources, or past experience. Use the audit to identify the most useful sources.

Four ways to make sure the information reaches your competitor analysis group are:

1. Set up in-house "competitor intelligence" seminars and include representatives from all departments.
2. Make sure employees who pass on valuable information are rewarded, either financially or through a commendation.

. . . .

Information Key

Think about three positions that your company will be filling in the near future. Who is likely to apply for these spots? What competitor information might they have that could be extracted either during the interview or after they are hired?

1. Position _____ Information _____

_____

_____

2. Position _____ Information _____

_____

_____

3. Position _____ Information _____

_____

_____

. . . .

3. Keep employees informed about how specific bits of competitor data have benefited the company.

4. Acknowledge all information contributed by employees even if it does not prove to be useful.

Reverse Engineering

"You should know your competitors' products as well as you know your own," is how one design engineer puts it. Have your technicians continually tear apart competing products to examine not only materials and specifications, but evidence of new production techniques, new suppliers of components, and improved technology.

Reverse engineering is a legitimate and useful means of keeping up on your competitors. When Advanced Energy Technology, Inc., patented a new speed reduction gear, the company immediately received numerous orders for one or two of the items. The buyers: the firm's principal competitors.

The Bridgestone Corp. had a U.S. representative purchase samples of every new tire introduced by Goodyear, Goodrich, and other American manufacturers. The products were sent to Bridgestone's headquarters and examined in detail. Since this Japanese competitor was thoroughly prepared when it entered the U.S. market, it captured a significant portion of tire sales in the United States.

Again, don't neglect the obvious. A food processor was considering cutting costs by replacing maple syrup with corn syrup in one of its products. In calculating how the new formula would compare with the competitor's brand, engineers found that the competitor had already made the switch. How could they have gained this important information earlier? Simply by reading the list of ingredients on the competitor's package. Another often overlooked source is serial numbers on competitor products. Checked periodically, they could reveal a company's rate of sales.

Reverse engineering need not stop with the product itself. One researcher, by examining the label on boxes in which a competitor shipped his goods, was able to identify the supplier of the packaging. A simple query to the box company uncovered the number of boxes sold to the competitor each month. This enabled the rival firm to estimate the company's production.

Technicians will be able to spot important details while conducting reverse engineering. But here are some overall questions to ask:

In what ways is the product superior to our comparable model?
In what ways is it inferior?
How has the competitor incorporated cost savings?
What is the significance of his use of different materials?
Is the competitor's product easier to install or maintain?
Is it more reliable, precise, durable?

. . . .

Action Probes

Have you done head-to-head comparison testing of your products against comparable competitor models in order to uncover and exploit your strengths?

Are there flaws in competitors' products that you can detect and publicize to customers?

. . . .

COMPETITIVE ANALYSIS WORKSHEET 4

IN-HOUSE COMPETITOR INFORMATION AUDIT

Department _____ Date _____

Dept. Representative _____ Title _____

1. What specific types of competitive information does your department need?

_____

_____

_____

2. In what ways would this information help you to do your job better?

_____

_____

_____

3. Do any of the employees of your department have sources of competitor information in the following areas:

____ Former employee of competitor company

____ Personal or professional contacts with current personnel of competitor

____ Contacts with competitors' customers

____ Contacts with competitors' suppliers

____ Contacts with others who have competitive information (e.g., consultants, lawyers, acountants)

____ Membership in professional or trade organizations

____ Attendance at conventions, conferences, trade fairs, and so forth

____ General industry contacts

____ Other sources: _____

4. List the names of these people and your estimate of the frequency with which they can supply competitive data:

Name	Position	Type of Source	Frequently/ Occasionally/ Sporadically/
_____	_____	_____	_____
_____	_____	_____	_____
_____	_____	_____	_____
_____	_____	_____	_____

5. Have employees of your department been informed of the importance of passing along competitive information?

___ Yes   ___ No

Do they know to whom they should report this information?

___ Yes   ___ No

Have you put in place a system for evaluating and reporting such information?

___ Yes   ___ No

6. In what areas do you feel your department can contribute to our company's knowledge of competitors?

_____

_____

7. Other than employees listed in 4, what sources of competitor information could be developed through your department?

_____

_____

8. How can information gathered by your department on competitors be put to the best use?

_____

_____

6

How to Gather Information from Competitor and Trade Sources

Competitors themselves often prove to be valuable sources of information on which to base your analysis. Every company, while trying to keep plans and activities secret from rivals, inevitably reveals a great deal of information in the course of its business. In many cases you won't need to steal or buy a competitor's secrets because he will give them away for free. Competitive Analysis Worksheet 5 at the end of this chapter gives you a handy tool to make sure you're taking full advantage of this valuable information. It will help you to check on and organize the many facets of his business that the competitor reveals every day.

Direct Inquiry

Many companies have no systematic policy on what employees are allowed to reveal to outsiders. An engineer of a large shipbuilding firm sent a researcher confidential plans on the redesign of an important propeller simply because he was asked for them. Secretaries and receptionists may give out detailed information about their companies' activities.

For example, a switchboard operator at a company that manufactured machinery for the shoe industry told a reporter that the company's president wouldn't be able to talk to him. He and several other top managers, she said, had rushed to Ohio to try to solve the production problems at the company's main plant. The reporter, in the course of another conversation, passed this potentially significant piece of news on to one of the firm's competitors.

One of your competitor's maintenance engineers might be willing to discuss his firm's use of replacement parts, not realizing that the information could be used to calculate machine usage. Public relations and marketing managers may, in the course of boasting of a new product or coming advertising campaign, reveal more information than they intend.

Since competitors are likely to be on guard when talking directly to

. . . .

Information Key

List two facts that you would like to know about specific competitors. Then think of someone within that company who might supply you with the information. Contact the person yourself or through an intermediary and see if you're right.

Fact: _____

Source: _____

Fact: _____

Source: _____

. . . .

another company in their business, you will usually want to make such information requests through third parties. These may be professional research companies or neutral firms with which your company does business—consultants, accountants, suppliers. In some cases, companies hire consultants to conduct an industry study. The consultant requests detailed information from key competing firms. A report containing generalized industry figures is issued to all participants in the study. But company-specific facts are channeled only to the client.

Use Section A of Competitive Analysis Worksheet 5 to keep a record of valuable information sources within a competitive firm.

Observation

"You never know where you're going to pick up a piece of the puzzle," says Information Data Search president Leonard Fuld. "Go out and look at the competitor's plant. Count the number of parking spaces and you'll have a good idea of his work force. Telephone the factory at night to see if he's added an extra shift."

A Japanese company estimated the rate of business done by competitors by measuring the level of rust on rail tracks leading to their plants. A paper-making firm was able to estimate the effect of a competitor's plant modernization by hiring engineers and architects to study the plant from the outside.

Direct observation is a simple and inexpensive way to gather competitive information. For example, you might use it to determine:

Who a competitor's suppliers are

Its stockpile of raw materials

Details about plant construction and layout

Manufacturing or processing techniques

Size and frequency of shipments of finished goods

Visits to Facilities

Some companies offer plant tours to the public. By sending knowledgeable employees to take these tours, you can uncover important information about competitors' operations—manufacturing methods, new machinery used, quality control techniques, automation strategies.

Companies in retail or other businesses in which facilities are open to the public should make regular inspections of the competitors' premises. What new merchandising or display ideas is the firm using? How has it increased service or cut costs? In any business, having someone play the role of potential customer can be revealing. How effective are the firm's sales and marketing efforts? Which product advantages are emphasized? How aggressively does the competitor pursue new accounts?

Record the results of your direct observation and facilities' visits in Section B of Competitive Analysis Worksheet 5. Note whether the information was obtained from a single visit or from surveillance of one or more days.

· ·

Information Key

Assume the role of a first-time customer who knows nothing about your firm or your principal competitor. What would be your first impression of each company?

Your company: _____

_____

_____

Your competitor: _____

_____

_____

· ·

Speeches

Company executives are increasingly being called upon to give speeches. These can be revealing. Often, the executive will illustrate points with examples taken from his own company's experience. In addition, speeches will often reveal something about management's philosophy and assumptions. A recognized source of information about speeches given by executives of publicly held firms is the *Wall Street Transcript* (120 Wall Street, New York, NY 10005), which covers presentations to security analysts and reproduces many speeches verbatim.

A good example of the type of information that can be found in speeches occurred at a major chemical company. Planners observed that the chief executive of a competing firm had given several speeches emphasizing the slow sales in the field and the need to cut costs. This helped to convince them that the competitor held pessimistic assumptions about the market and was not likely to add capacity soon. It contributed to this company's decision to expand a plant to meet the growth in demand that they themselves were expecting.

In January 1985, Black & Decker Corp. president and chief executive Laurence J. Farley addressed the 75th annual meeting of shareholders. A competitor who was trying to fill in a picture of Black & Decker would have been able to extract the following points:

1. Emphasis on the Black & Decker brand name and three strategic goals.
2. Emphasis on return on investment as a criterion of success and dissatisfaction with current level.
3. Details of new product introductions.
4. Importance of recently acquired household products division of company.
5. Strategy for expanding international business.
6. Corporate philosophy change from product orientation to marketing orientation.

Chief executives are not the only managers who give speeches. Engineers address scientific forums and may reveal specific details about product development strategies. Sales managers speak before trade meetings—they may mention forecasts or marketing plans. Financial officers talk to professional groups and may discuss their companies' controls or experiences. You should not just track and review all of these speeches, you should analyze them in depth, isolating revealing points and incorporating them into your analysis. Part C of Competitive Analysis Worksheet 5 will enable you to compile a list of competitors' managers who have spoken in public and who may in the future provide further information.

Company Publications

Almost every company issues some publications—employee newsletters, accounts of the company's history, fact books, public relations, and educational material. All these may contain valuable competitor information. Most are available on request.

If you are not aware of all the publications that your competitors put out, the reference work *Corporate Publications In Print* (McGraw-Hill, Inc., 1221 Avenue of the Americas, New York, NY 10019) should be able to help you.

Another type of publication that you shouldn't neglect is product operating manuals. "A considerable amount of competitor information can be gained by having engineers study operating manuals," says Information Data Search president Leonard Fuld. "These books are often extremely detailed."

Part D of Competitive Analysis Worksheet 5 gives you a place to list the publications of competitors. It will help you evaluate them and make sure you are up-to-date on all publications listed.

Press Releases

Companies issue press releases for many reasons: to announce a new product, to make known a management change, to detail the settlement of a lawsuit, to outline joint ventures, or to tell about a major new account. Not all these events are important enough to be picked up by the press, but they may be of significant interest to direct competitors. Make sure that you are on a mailing list to receive this information on a timely basis.

Here are some examples of information taken from actual press releases:

1. Analogic, a manufacturer of electronic equipment, announced the formation of a subsidiary to sell a wide range of equipment through catalogs.

   Competitor interest: New distribution channels.
2. Borg-Warner, a large industrial company, announced a management realignment, including important promotions among top executives.

Competitor interest: Possible clues to change in management direction.

3. Hazeltine Corp. outlined the licensing of its AM stereo radio technology to Sony Corp.

    Competitor interest: An example of Hazeltine's product development strategy.

4. Penril, a diversified technology company, detailed an agreement with Graybar Electric Co. for the latter to begin distributing Penril's modems and multiplexers.

    Competitor interest: New distribution channel.

Investor Information

If your competitors are publicly held companies, you can obtain a great deal of important data from the information that they distribute to investors. In the United States, the Securities and Exchange Commission (SEC) requires all firms that sell stock to the public to meet very specific disclosure requirements. This information is contained not only in the reports sent regularly to investors, but also in filings forwarded to the SEC and available on request from that body.

Annual reports give general financial information for the most recent and past fiscal years, including earnings, cash flow, and balance sheet data. But they also include a discussion by the company's management of the progress of various business segments. The best way to extract information is to examine the current report in relation to past years' reports, seeking trends and changes in emphasis.

General Electric, for example, started a research effort in the area of solid state controls for appliances after competitors Whirlpool and Hitachi both emphasized the devices in their annual reports.

Some questions that your competitors' annual reports might answer include:

Which segments does management consider most important?

Have interest payments on the firm's debt increased significantly?

Information Key

Assemble some sample press releases from a major competitor. Read through them and see if a pattern emerges. Can you detect any messages by reading "between the lines"? Record your observations here:

_____

_____

_____

_____

What patterns emerge in the company's capital spending?

Are significant litigation or contingencies discussed in the footnotes?

Who are the firm's accountants, suppliers, consultants, and so forth?

What important acquisitions have been made in the past year?

Information Key

Go through the annual report of a major competitor and try to pick out three competitive weaknesses revealed in either the narrative or financial section. List them below.

1. _____

2. _____

3. _____

Quarterly reports give information similar to annual reports, but in a highly abbreviated form. They can enable you to keep posted on developments throughout the year.

Proxy statements give information to shareholders who wish to turn over their voting rights to management. They can serve as a source of data, such as:

The age, occupation, and background of the firm's directors

The compensation levels of top executives

Stock ownership of managers

Bonus, incentive, and retirement plans

Form 10-K is a more detailed version of the annual report, as filed with the SEC. The following example illustrates the type of detailed information often contained in the 10-K.

. . . .

Competitor Data from Form 10-K

Marsh Supermarkets, Inc., operates 74 supermarkets and 142 convenience stores in Indiana and Ohio. The following are a few of the facts that a competitor could have learned from the company's form 10-K for the year ending March, 1984.

The average square footage of Marsh's supermarkets was 26,000.

48 percent of supermarket space was new or had been remodeled in the past five years.

Two years ago, Marsh acquired a warehouse that had been built in 1969. It has 409,000 square feet of space, 131,000 square feet of it refrigerated. The property contains 44 acres.

Selling margins last year were 21 percent of sales, operating expenses 20 percent of sales. Sales increased 6.5 percent, but 2.4 percent was gain due to inflation.

. . . .

Special material, such as a proxy statement in relation to a merger or other major organizational change, or a prospectus describing the issuance of new securities, provides a great deal of information about a company's operations and finances.

The easiest way to make sure you receive investor information is to buy a few shares of the competitor's stock. As you receive documents, check them off in Section G of Competitive Analysis Worksheet

5 and examine them thoroughly. Here are a few examples of potentially useful information for a competitor culled from investor material:

> Black & Decker plans a major advertising campaign for its new housewares line, with promotional spending exceeding the amount spent by the entire industry in the previous year.

> Veeco Instruments intends to expand its Dallas robotics plant in the coming year and open new facilities in Israel and Japan.

> Sealed Power is phasing in a new system to connect its distribution centers by computer.

Advertisements and Promotional Material

These sources can provide a great deal of significant information easily and at no cost, such as:

> Which products are competitors pushing?

> Which features do they emphasize?

> What markets are they trying to reach?

> What are their products' specifications?

A study of competitors' advertising can sometimes provide an interesting perspective on the competitive landscape. For example, in the field of office automation systems, Wang Laboratories ran a series of advertisements that listed the attributes of its VS system alongside those of the IBM 36. Besides the direct comparison, the copy contained the clear message: "We're gunning for IBM." In addition to the information on the capabilities of the VS, this advertising would indicate to a competitor the exact positioning of the system and the competitive focus of Wang's marketers.

Data General countered these ads with almost identical spots that featured its ability to "deliver today what IBM and Wang promise tomorrow." Charts compared features of Data General's MV product against the IBM System 36 and the Wang VS model. A competitor

· ·

Information Key

Take one of your own advertisements and those for similar products of two competitors. What does each tell about the company's perception of its market position and product advantages?

Yours: _____

_____

_____

Competitor 1: _____

_____

_____

Competitor 2: _____

_____

_____

· ·

might ask: Is Wang ignoring a strong challenge from Data General? Is Data General trying to catch up to two industry leaders? Are both competitors making a mistake by trying to fit into an overly crowded niche?

Sometimes where a competitor advertises can be as significant as what the ads say. A company buying space in a national magazine is clearly trying to reach a mass market. A hand tool maker who runs spots mainly in retail trade publications probably sees chain store buyers as more important customers than end-users.

Promotional material, such as product description brochures and technical manuals, can provide you with information ranging from product specifications to delivery schedules, from performance expectations to product selling points. Be sure to collect as much of this information as possible and to study it for potential competitive advantages.

Figure 4 is an example of an advertisement that appeared in *Purchasing* magazine. Besides an overview of Morris, Wheeler's capabilities, a competitor could observe that the company seems to see its competitive advantages in large inventory and processing quality rather than in, for example, speed of delivery.

Use Section H of Competitive Analysis Worksheet 5 to evaluate your competitors' advertising and promotional material. Remember to track this area regularly to spot trends and changes in emphasis.

Help-Wanted Ads

Competitors often tip their hands about both current and future operations when they advertise for prospective employees. A few examples

---

At Morris, Wheeler, our service center is not just a warehouse. By offering you a full range of processing and fabricating capabilities, our service center is a one-stop steel resource center that can save you time and money.

Vast Inventory

We start with one of the region's largest steel inventories. Morris, Wheeler warehouses a wide range of stock shapes from bars, plates, and sheets to square and rectangular structural tubing, boiler tubes, welded grating, expanded metal, and a full spectrum of structurals—from "C" to "Z." Whatever you need, chances are we have it—and can get it to you *now.*

Made-to-Order

But our inventory is only the beginning. It's what we *do* with steel that's won the loyalty of Morris, Wheeler's customers for over 150 years. Our large-capacity KV-6 saw cuts to extremely close tolerances. We give you intricate burning with a whistle-clean edge. We burn conical holes and do three-phase (dimensional) flame cutting. Punching, forming, coping, welding—these are all routine at Morris, Wheeler. Drawing, rolling, stress relieving—we do that, too. We also do heat treating, grit and shot blasting, and painting. And every piece of steel we process is handled to our exacting specifications. Our quality program meets all industry standards.

Figure 4. Sample Advertisement

....

Action Probes

Could you upgrade your promotional material in order to give your sales reps an advantage over those of competitors when they approach customers?

Are competitors ignoring a key selling point in their ads that you could exploit in yours to win customers?

Should you run direct competitive ads refuting claims made by competitors?

....

will illustrate the type of information that you can pick up by regularly reviewing listings:

An ad for sales reps highlighted McDonnell Douglas Information Systems Group's rapidly growing computer-aided design business. The text listed eight cities where openings for sales reps existed. It named the main industries to which the service would be marketed (architectural, engineering, and construction). And it gave an estimate of the sales for the group during the coming year.

Polaroid Corp., in a help-wanted ad seeking researchers, pointed out the importance of its electronic imaging business and gave details of four major areas of research.

Atlantic Scientific Corp. disclosed its market penetration program, yearly sales, and approximate number of employees when advertising for a director of marketing.

Personnel advertisements can also give clues to production problems and quality control difficulties as competitors seek help in those areas.

Section 4 of Competitive Analysis Worksheet 5 will help you to keep track of these advertisements. The publications you cover will depend on the location of competitors and their habits in advertising for employees.

Trade Sources

Trade sources often provide competitor information because, unlike general organizations and publications, they are focused on your industry and your areas of concern.

Trade and Professional Organizations

Through the meetings, seminars, and newsletters of these groups, your employees are likely to contact both their counterparts from competitor companies and other industry participants. Information is exchanged and an alert employee looking for competitor data can pick up useful facts.

It is also a good idea to develop close relations with the officials and staff of trade groups. Since they have contact with most of the companies in the industry, they may be able to fill you in on market trends or even specific competitor plans.

Trade associations exist for almost every industry and for many market segments. Encourage your people to take an active role in any such organizations that deal with your industry. Regularly review with them the information-gathering techniques covered in the last chapter.

Professional groups can also serve as sources of competitor data. Make sure that your employees take part in those groups that are applicable as well.

Part A of Competitive Analysis Worksheet 6 gives you a tool for keeping track of which employees are involved in trade and professional groups. Once you've compiled a complete list, you can refer to it when looking for particular types of data and ask the organization member from your company to search out the information or recommend contacts.

Three publications will help you to locate specific trade and professional organizations:

National Trade and Professional Associations of the U.S.

Columbia Books, Inc.
777 14th Street NW
Washington, DC 20005

Encyclopedia of Associations

Gale Research Co.
Book Tower
Detroit, MI 48226

World Guide to Trade Associations

R.R. Bowker Co.
1180 Avenue of the Americas
New York, NY 10036

Trade Publications

Because these are one of the most fertile sources of information on
your competitors and industry, you should examine them in detail, not
just read them. For example, statistics and diagrams that appeared in
the magazine *Progressive Grocer* showed not only the exact layout of
a supermarket chain's store, but the cost of the facility and its initial
inventory, the weekly sales volume, and a profile of the market served.
All of this data could be useful to a direct competitor of that chain.

Below is a brief list of the trade and professional publications available. There are many others. You should be interested in following
ones that deal with closely related industries as well as those directly
concerned with your own.

Air Transport World	Iron Age
Automotive News	Journal of Retailing
Bank Marketing	Paper Trade Journal
The CPA Journal	Personnel Administrator
Electronic Business	Plastics World
Forest Industries	Restaurant Business
Hotel & Motel Management	Textile Industries

Action Probes

Are you using trade publications not only as sources of competitor information but as sources of ideas, new operating techniques, and industry trends?

Could you better use trade groups and publications to enhance your company's reputation or attract customers (e.g., by becoming more visible in trade group seminars, by encouraging employees to write articles for publications)?

Part B of Competitive Analysis Worksheet 6 helps you record all the trade publications that your company receives. The person in your company who is most familiar with the topic should be assigned to review each publication every time it appears, and to pass on any valuable competitor or market information to the competitor analysis group.

Trade Shows and Exhibitions

Trade shows are an excellent source of information on competitors' new products. They also give your employees a chance to make contact with a wide range of potential sources of information. Emphasize to those employees that they should be alert to every nuance of a competitor's presentation, as well as to developing trends in the industry as a whole.

For example, a consumer products firm's manager of packaging attended a trade show featuring new packaging machinery. He observed a direct competitor's representative taking a great deal of interest in a high-speed computerized packaging machine. He reported this to his superiors, indicating that it might mean the competitor was planning a plant expansion. Further investigation proved this to be the case.

Part C of Competitive Analysis Worksheet 6 is designed to organize your coverage of trade shows and exhibitions. Make sure that someone from your company covers all relevant shows, even if the company itself is not participating. This is also a good place to pick up product literature and to find out about introduction schedules for new products.

COMPETITIVE ANALYSIS WORKSHEET 5

COMPETITOR SOURCES: CHECKLIST

Reproduce this checklist and use one copy for each major competitor.

A. Direct Inquiry

Which of the competitor's employees have been or could be used as sources of information?

Employee	Position	Phone No.	Used/Not Used	Actual or Potential Information Category
_____	_____	_____	_____	_____
_____	_____	_____	_____	_____
_____	_____	_____	_____	_____
_____	_____	_____	_____	_____

B. Observation/Facility Visits

Facility 1: _____

Plant tour/visit is available	____	Has been taken ____
One-time inspection has been made	____	Follow-up on (date) _____
Surveillance has been conducted	____	Follow-up on (date) _____

Information obtained through observation:

_____

_____

_____

Facility 2: _____

Plant tour/visit is available _____ Has been taken _____
One-time inspection has been made _____ Follow-up on (date) _____
Surveillance has been conducted _____ Follow-up on (date) _____
Information obtained through observation:

_____

_____

C. Speeches

List competitor employees who frequently give speeches:

Employee	Position	Speaks before (Group)	Competitor Information (Much/Some/None)
_____	_____	_____	_____
_____	_____	_____	_____
_____	_____	_____	_____
_____	_____	_____	_____

D. Company Publications

Publication	When Issued	Value as Source (High/Medium/Low)
_____	_____	_____
_____	_____	_____
_____	_____	_____
_____	_____	_____

E. Press Releases

Are we on the competition's mailing list for all press releases?

_____ Yes   _____ No

How valuable are these documents?

_____ Very   _____ Somewhat   _____ Not valuable

F. Investor Information

Source _____ Useful for (type of information) _____

Annual report   _____

Quarterly reports   _____

Proxy material   _____

Form 10K   _____

Special material   _____

Other_____ _____

G. Advertisements

General advertising:

Media _____ Target market _____

Revealing content _____

Product 1 _____:

Media _____ Target market _____

Revealing content _____

Product 2 _____:

Media _____ Target market _____

Revealing content _____

Do we have all available brochures and product manuals on competitors' products?

_____ Yes   _____ No

H. Help-Wanted Ads

Do we systematically cover all the competitors' personnel advertisements?

_____ Yes   _____ No

In which media do they frequently appear?

_____

Do they usually reveal significant information?

_____ Yes   _____ No

Examples: _____

_____

COMPETITIVE ANALYSIS WORKSHEET 6

TRADE SOURCES: CHECKLIST

A. Trade and Professional Organizations

Group	In-House Contact	Group Official/ Source	Type of Information
_____	_____	_____	_____
_____	_____	_____	_____
_____	_____	_____	_____
_____	_____	_____	_____

B. Trade Publications

Publication	Reviewed by	When Issued	Type of Information
_____	_____	_____	_____
_____	_____	_____	_____
_____	_____	_____	_____
_____	_____	_____	_____

C. Trade Shows and Exhibitions

Show	Date	In-House Contact	Type of Information
_____	_____	_____	_____
_____	_____	_____	_____
_____	_____	_____	_____
_____	_____	_____	_____

7

How to Gather Information from Published and Government Sources

Magazines, newspapers, books, newsletters, and industry reports—all can serve as useful sources for competitive information. They are particularly useful in helping you build a statistical and factual base for your ongoing analysis. They tend to be more precise and quantitative than field sources, and are easily accessible. Their main disadvantage is that they are not as current. Even the facts in a daily newspaper may have already been circulating by word of mouth before appearing in print and will have lost some of their competitive value.

Here are some tips on making the best use of the many published sources of information available to you:

1. Recognize limitations. Are the facts up-to-date? Are they inclusive? Accurate?

2. Distinguish fact from opinion. Most articles and books will show signs of the author's biases and preconceptions.

3. Use libraries. However extensive your company library, you can tap a much wider range of sources by using public research libraries, particularly those of business colleges.

4. When using a published source, note all relevant information. For example, you may be reading an article to gain an idea of a competitor's sales level, but also come across information on his research program.

Note that different countries will have different sources, in both numbers and extent of information. Use the suggestions and names in this manual as a starting point for your research.

Bibliographic Works

There are so many reference works, reports, and statistical surveys available that your first step should be to consult books which will guide you to the information sources you need. These bibliographic works will help you to avoid time-consuming searches through numerous directories and reference works. They may also point you toward specific and pertinent information sources that you would otherwise overlook.

Fill in the names of the most useful bibliographic references you can find in Part A of Competitive Analysis Worksheet 7 at the end of this chapter. Note what information they have successfully directed you to, and use them when needed in the future.

Below are a few bibliographic guides. Additional works are listed in the Appendix. Check your local university business school library for more, as well as major business publishers in your region.

Business Information Sources

University of California Press
223 Fulton Street
Berkeley, CA 94720

How to Find Information about Companies

Washington Researchers, Ltd.
918 16th St. NW
Washington, DC 20006

World Sources of Market Information

Gower Publishing Co.
Aldershot, Hants
England

Directory of Industry Data Sources

Ballinger Publishing Co.
Cambridge, MA 02138

Marketing Information: A Professional Reference Guide

Business Publishing Division
College of Business Administration
Georgia State University
Atlanta, GA 30303

Directories

While directories do not usually contain exhaustive information about particular companies, they do serve as useful sources of the basic facts about competitors. They can help you identify potential competitors when you are contemplating moving into new markets. They are also good sources for learning about possible suppliers and customers. Directories list companies according to size, industry, or geographic territory. Begin your search for useful directories by consulting the *Directory of Directories* (Gale Research Co., Book Tower, Detroit, MI 48226). List the ones you find helpful in Part B of Competitive Analysis Worksheet 7. Below are just a few examples of the types of directories available. See the Appendix for additional listings.

Million Dollar Directory

(160,000 U.S. companies with net worth over $500,000)

Principal International Businesses

(50,000 companies in 133 countries)

Europe's 10,000 Largest Companies

(8,000 industrials, 2,000 trading companies)
Dun's Marketing Services
3 Century Drive
Parsippany, NJ 07054

Japan Trade Directory

(2,000 Japanese companies)
Gale Research Co.
Book Tower
Detroit, MI 48226

American Export Register

(U.S. companies doing business abroad)
Thomas International Publishing Co.

One Penn Plaza
New York, NY 10001

Directory of Corporate Affiliates
(parent companies and subsidiaries)
National Register Publishing Co.
5201 Old Orchard Rd.
Skokie, IL 60077

Other Reference Works

The number of reference works available—on particular markets, industries, trade, financial statistics, raw materials, production capacity, government regulations, technology trends, consumer preferences, safety, economic climate, and a host of other subjects—is practically endless. Select and use the ones that are most pertinent to your market and competitive information needs. But keep in mind three limitations of all reference works:

Because of the time required to compile and print information, even the most current editions of reference books will be dated.

The averages and aggregate data contained in reference works may prove useful as comparisons, but they can also be misleading. Your particular segment of the market or your geographic area may not fit the pattern.

Many studies, especially those covering private companies, are based on the reports of the companies themselves. Business owners may not be entirely candid in their replies and the resulting data may be inaccurate.

Use Part C of Worksheet 7 to compile a list of reference works that you've found helpful. Include those most commonly used in your company library, consulting others in research libraries when needed. The following list gives a cross-section of the types of reference books available.

Automobile International (Johnston International Pub. Co.)—a yearly report on auto production and export

Chemical Economics Handbook (Stanford Research Inst.)—a survey of the international chemical market

Concise Guide to International Markets (International Advertising Assn.)—data on marketing in 100 markets worldwide

European Marketing Data & Statistics (Gale Research)—comparison data on markets in 26 countries

Exporter's Encyclopedia (Dun's Marketing Services)—information on exporting to 220 world markets

50,000 Leading U.S. Companies (News Front)—sales, number of plants, and financial data on public and private firms

International Marketing Data and Statistics (Gale Research)—comparisons of markets in 100 countries in Asia, Africa, and South America

Reference Book of Corporate Managements (Dun's Marketing Services)—biographical data on 200,000 officers and directors

Sources of Financial Information (Robert Morris Associates)—where to find specific industry financial data

Periodicals

Careful perusal of the general press, business and financial press, and trade publications will provide you with information on specific competitors, your markets and industry, and the general trade affecting your competitive climate.

Japanese firms have literally made a science of studying these information sources. Mitsubishi International Corp., for example, occupies two floors of the Pan Am Building in New York and employs an army of researchers to comb general, trade, and technical periodicals for information. The company operates its own microfilming service and compiles extensive indexes and cross-references. No mention of a competitor move is likely to slip through this net.

Information Key

Consider three reference works that you use regularly. Rate each one according to how pertinent it is, how current the information is, and how convenient the form of presentation is. Keep these criteria in mind as you rate sources in the Analysis Worksheet.

	Very	Somewhat	Not at All
How good is the likelihood that it contains the data you're looking for?			
Source 1 _____	____	____	____
Source 2 _____	____	____	____
Source 3 _____	____	____	____

	Very	Somewhat	Not at All
How up-to-date is the data?			
Source 1	____	____	____
Source 2	____	____	____
Source 3	____	____	____
Is the form in which the data is presented convenient?			
Source 1	____	____	____
Source 2	____	____	____
Source 3	____	____	____

. . . .

One frequently overlooked source of competitor data is the local newspaper in the city where a company has its headquarters or major plants. These publications are likely to cover news and events that don't reach newspapers of wider circulation. A few of the pieces of data having competitive interest that you are likely to pick up are:

Hiring or layoffs of workers

Fires and accidents

Awards of major contracts or significant new business

Changes in management, especially promotions of plant managers, sales managers, etc.

Plant expansions or closings

Part D of Competitive Analysis Worksheet 7 helps you organize your coverage of periodicals to make sure that each one is examined in depth. Sometimes you will want to consult a wider range of periodicals in order to conduct research on a particular topic. For this, indexes of periodicals are helpful. You should also consult these indexes regularly in order to:

Check all references to principal competitors

Identify additional periodicals that you should be subscribing to

Uncover important articles on industry trends and markets

Below are a few of the more important periodical indexes:

Business Periodicals Index

H.W. Wilson Co.
950 University Ave.
Bronx, NY 10452

Financial Times Index

London Times Business
   Information Ltd.
Bracken House
London EC 4P 4B4
England

F&S Index Europe
F&S Index International

Predicasts, Inc.
11001 Cedar Ave.
Cleveland, Ohio 44106

Wall Street Journal Index
Dow Jones & Co., Inc.
200 Liberty St.
New York, NY 10281

Clipping Services

Many companies use clipping services to cover a wider range of periodicals than they could using their own resources. These services will
search through publications looking for particular references—to
companies, products, and so forth. They charge a monthly fee plus a
certain amount per item forwarded.

When used in a general way, clipping services have several draw-
backs. First, they are likely to send you a great deal of redundant information—many stories that give the same details about a
competitor's routine product announcement, for example. In addition,
since they do not review or organize the clippings, they still leave a
great deal of work to be done by you—sorting, analysis, and so forth.

The best way to use clipping services is to have them conduct
specific research. You may want them to track only a competitor's
help-wanted advertisements, or check the reaction to a particular, innovative product, or gather information on a company that is considering entering your market.

A few prominent clipping services are:

Burrelle's Press Clipping Services

75 East Northfield Ave.
Livingston, NJ 07039

Packaged Facts

247 Madison Ave.
New York, NY 10016

ATP Clipping Bureau

5 Beekman St.
New York, NY 10038

Bacon's Clipping Bureau

14 East Jackson Blvd.
Chicago, IL 60604

Electronic Data Base Sources

Because of the large volume and unwieldy nature of written information, more and more companies have begun to use electronic data bases as a quicker and more effective research tool. These services provide the text or an abstract of articles and reports by means of computer display terminals. In some cases, you can tap the data base directly, ordering the information that you want. In others, an intermediary scans the available information and fills your request.

There are hundreds of data bases. Some, like the New York Times Information Bank and the Dow-Jones News Retrieval Database, cover general and business news. Others accumulate information on one subject or industry, such as the petroleum or copper industries. Data base vendors supply the actual computer links that make the data bases available.

This field is growing so rapidly that you will need to consult a reference work in order to pinpoint the organizations and particular data bases that might be useful for your research. Some guides currently on the market are:

Encyclopedia of Information Systems and Services

Gale Research Co.
Book Tower
Detroit, MI 48226

Information Industry Market Place

R.R. Bowker Co.
1180 Avenue of the Americas
New York, NY 10036

Annual Directory

Information Industry Association
316 Pennsylvania Ave.
Washington, DC 20003

Part E of Competitive Analysis Worksheet 7 is for listing and analyzing some of the data base sources that you think might be useful for your competitive analysis effort. Because of the expense involved, cost effectiveness is a key factor in selection.

University Sources

Professors and students of business administration frequently conduct detailed studies of companies and industries. Some of this research can be valuable in competitor analysis.

Locating pertinent studies is becoming easier as more and more clearinghouses begin publishing listings of case studies and offering copies for sale, usually for a nominal fee to cover costs. The *Intercollegiate Case Clearinghouse* (Soldiers Field Post Office, Boston, MA 02163) publishes a regularly updated bibliography of case studies conducted at many different colleges. The organization can also direct you to similar clearinghouses in other parts of the world.

Harvard Business School puts out the *Harvard Business School Case Collection* directory. There is no question that companies that are competing with the firms mentioned in these studies could obtain valuable information by studying the reports. For information, write: HBS Case Services, Morgan Hall, Harvard Business School, Boston, MA 02163.

Use Part F of Competitive Analysis Worksheet 7 to check off any applicable case studies that you use in your competitive analysis. Be sure to keep up-to-date on the latest reports available, as the information in the studies will become dated quickly. But even historical studies can give clues to the operating procedures and decision-making processes of a competitor's management.

Government Sources

Practically every government in the world is in the business of collecting information. Much of this data is used for the government's own purposes—estimating revenues, controlling trade, regulating the marketplace. Other information is collected and compiled in order to aid companies headquartered or doing business in the country. Almost all of it is available at little or no cost. You should not overlook it as a source of data on your competitors and markets. Many of the facts in the following discussion of U.S. government sources of information apply to the governments of other countries as well.

Federal Government

Cabinet departments and the 27 major regulatory agencies in the U.S. government can provide a wealth of competitor and market data. These range from broad statistics to very specific studies of particular markets and situations.

To gain general information about the information available, write to *Superintendent of Documents,* U.S. Government Printing Office, Washington, DC 20406. Specify your particular area of interest.

The Department of Commerce is the largest compiler of business data in the federal government. For example, every five years it issues a *Census of Manufacturers.* Special studies based on the same data are released continually. In these works you can find information as detailed as the number of companies in Cleveland, Ohio, which produce fabricated structural metal products and have more than 20 employees (23 companies). Concentration studies indicate the percent of business controlled by the leading firms in various product groups. The census is supplemented by similar studies in service industries, transportation firms, and retail companies.

The Commerce Department's research is not limited to domestic businesses. Its Industry and Trade Administration publishes detailed *Country Market Surveys.* Figure 5 is an abbreviated sample of the type of data contained in these studies, this one conducted in Hong Kong several years ago.

Other agencies of the federal government have available specialty information on a wide variety of subjects. A few examples:

Library of Congress. Its National Reference Center can put you in touch with university experts who are involved in government-sponsored research.

Geological Survey. Its aerial photographs and detailed maps can be useful in studying a competitor's facilities.

Internal Revenue Service. Publishes summaries of corporate tax returns.

Interstate Commerce Commission. Conducts studies of transportation economics.

Bureau of Labor Statistics. Wage and productivity data for various areas of the country.

Patent and Trademark Office. Weekly listings and abstracts of patents filed.

Part A of Competitive Analysis Worksheet 8 gives you an organizer for government information available from your national government. Make sure all new studies and statistics are reviewed on a timely basis.

Freedom of Information Act

The FOIA requires the U.S. government to release to anyone making a request any documents in any government file. Of the 70,000 requests for information each year, most are commercially motivated—

III. THE APPAREL INDUSTRY IN HONG KONG

The clothing industry is Hong Kong's largest industry, and Hong Kong is the world's largest clothing exporter. This industry employs 32 percent of the industrial work force and supplies 40 percent of export revenue. Some 8,700 establishments are involved, averaging 27 workers per establishment.

Since government activity in economic matters is kept to a minimum, there is not a great deal of centrally available data; what there is appears in Table 2. In comparison to other countries, Hong Kong businesses are particularly secretive and do not usually report their production or cost figures to trade and similar associations. (According to the New York office of the Hong Kong Board of Trade, the last information on apparel production was published in 1974.) Nevertheless, excellent statistics are available on exports and imports; because Hong Kong's clothing industry is almost totally export-oriented, local production figures can be extrapolated from the trade figures.

The apparel industry has been the cornerstone of Hong Kong's economic development since World War II. Beginning with the concentration of emigrants from Shanghai, which has a tradition of industry experience, the garment industry in Hong Kong has grown almost exponentially until recently. This growth was based on two foundations: (1) the almost overnight immigration of a large adult population in the early 1970s, which created an infusion of human capital, and (2) a completely laissez-faire policy by the local government, coupled with a series of general worldwide tariff reductions.

Table 2. The Apparel Industry in Hong Kong
(U.S. $)

Number of firms	8,714 in 1977
	8,622 in 1976
Employment	239,058 in 1977
	223,419 in 1976
Apparel exports	$3.01 billion in 1977
	$3.05 billion in 1976
	$1.20 billion in 1972
Average wage rate	$1.05/hour
Average corporate tax rate	15%

Figure 5. A Brief Sample of an Industry Survey

Representative Apparel Manufacturers

KEE YIP GARMENTS MANUFAC-TURING CO. LTD. 7/F, Weel Town Industrial Building 13 Ko Fai Road, Yau Tong Bay Kowloon, Hong Kong Telephone: 3-418331-4	Men's and boys' outerwear jackets
GOODYEAR INDUSTRIAL COR-PORATION (Government Factory) 5B Arran Street, 7-9/F Kowloon, Hong Kong Telephone: 3-969266	Men's and boys' outerwear jackets
HARRY WICKING & COMPANY LTD. 28/F World Trade Centre Hong Kong Telephone: 5-799011	Men's and boys' overcoats
TRINITY CLOTHING LTD. Tal Building, 55 Austin Road Kowloon, Hong Kong Telephone: 12-212020	Men's and boys' suits
COMMONWEALTH GARMENT COMPANY LTD. 57 Hung To Road, 8-10/F Kowloon, Hong Kong Telephone: 3-896351	Women's and girls' coats
FOUR SEASONS GARMENTS Island House 2/F, 41J Ma Tau Wei Road Kowloon, Hong Kong Telephone: 3-640741, 3-623386	Women's and girls' suits
MANHATTAN GARMENTS LTD. Manhattan Building 2-16 Kwai Cheong Road Kwai Chung, New Territories Telephone: 12-246021-8	Trousers and shorts

Figure 5. Continued

companies trying to gain information about competitors. The data collected this way can be very valuable:

In 1977, the Food and Drug Administration released to Pfizer information about processes used by rival Hancock Labs.

In 1982, the Environmental Protection Agency made known to competitors Monsanto's confidential formula for the herbicide Round-up.

When the Interior Department awarded an $8 million contract to Control Data for computer services, Honeywell and Burroughs immediately requested details of the agreement in order to examine Control Data's capabilities and costs.

A Swedish ball-bearing maker gained copies of a Federal Trade Commission document that discussed Ingersoll-Rand's marketing tactics for bearings.

If you don't want to go to the trouble of locating and requesting FOIA data for yourself, an organization exists that will undertake the process for you. Contact: *FOI Services, Inc.,* 12315 Wilkins Ave., Rockville, MD 20852.

State or Regional Governments

Competitor information can be obtained from the agencies of the region where the company has its headquarters or plants, or in which it is incorporated. (Some companies incorporate outside their home areas to obtain favorable legal and tax conditions.)

For example, a researcher wanted to verify a rumor that a competitor in the apparel trade was planning to buy the plant and product line of a larger firm. He believed that the acquiring company would seek all possible financing for the transaction. So he went to the Industrial Development Authority in the state capital and verified the rumor. He was also able to uncover details such as the number of employees the company would hire, the value of the plant and equipment, and the start-up schedule, all of which the competitor had to reveal in order to apply for a state-backed loan.

. . . .

Information Key

You can best locate specific documents obtainable through the FOIA, or general studies that might be valuable, by examining the type of information and forms that you yourself have to file with the government. Review the documents required for census and regulatory purposes and identify three for which you would like to study corresponding competitor or industry data. List them here and follow up:

1. _____

2. _____

3. _____

. . . .

Use Part B of Competitive Analysis Worksheet 8 to create a checklist of information sources in your state or regional government. A few examples of the type of data to look for are:

A company's articles of incorporation

State labor and wage-level statistics

Uniform Commercial Code filings (financial information on companies that have borrowed against their assets)

Consumer complaints involving a company's products or service

Surveys of state manufacturers by commerce and economic development departments

Filings with food and drug regulation boards

Actions taken against companies by regulatory agencies

Local Government

Detailed information on companies is frequently available at the local level. For example, the Chamber of Commerce in the city where a competitor's plant is located can tell you about the area's economic and labor conditions. This will help you to estimate costs and resources. Officials of utilities can inform you of energy availability and cost, and may give you data on a competitor's usage. Developers of industrial tracts are good sources of information on competitor's expansion plans.

List local government and quasigovernment sources of information in Part C of Competitive Analysis Worksheet 8. Sources of competitor information include the following:

County or city clerks will have copies of deeds, mortgage data, local maps, zoning regulations and exemptions, and so forth.

Property appraisers or tax assessors will be familiar with the layout and value of industrial property

Building departments can provide copies of building permits.

The local planning board may have information on a competitor's expansion plans, including environmental impact studies, which can give good indications of production levels, processes, and so forth.

COMPETITIVE ANALYSIS WORKSHEET 7

PUBLISHED SOURCES: CHECKLIST

A. Bibliographic Reference Works

Title	Where Available	Type of Information

B. Directories

Title	Where Available	Type of Information

C. General Reference Works

Title	Where Available	Type of Information

D. Periodicals

Title	Frequency	Person Reviewing	Type of Information
_____	_____	_____	_____
_____	_____	_____	_____
_____	_____	_____	_____
_____	_____	_____	_____
_____	_____	_____	_____

E. Electronic Data Base Sources

Source	Originator	Vendor	Type of Information
_____	_____	_____	_____
_____	_____	_____	_____
_____	_____	_____	_____
_____	_____	_____	_____
_____	_____	_____	_____

F. University Sources

Study/Report	University	Date	Competitor Mentioned	Type of Information
_____	_____	_____	_____	_____
_____	_____	_____	_____	_____
_____	_____	_____	_____	_____
_____	_____	_____	_____	_____
_____	_____	_____	_____	_____

COMPETITIVE ANALYSIS WORKSHEET 8

For each level of government, list all possible sources of competitive information. Make sure that each is reviewed. Keep track of a person to contact within the agency in order to cut through red tape.

Agency	Competitor Information	Agency Contact	Reviewed by

A. National Level

_____ _____ _____ _____

_____ _____ _____ _____

_____ _____ _____ _____

_____ _____ _____ _____

_____ _____ _____ _____

B. State/Regional Level

_____ _____ _____ _____

_____ _____ _____ _____

_____ _____ _____ _____

_____ _____ _____ _____

_____ _____ _____ _____

C. Local Level

_____ _____ _____ _____

_____ _____ _____ _____

_____ _____ _____ _____

_____ _____ _____ _____

_____ _____ _____ _____

8

How to Gather Information from Third-Party Sources

"Any time money is exchanged, information is exchanged," says Information Data Search president Leonard Fuld. "Whether a competitor is buying materials, selling a product, borrowing capital, or hiring an employee, he is revealing something about his business. This is a good indication of where to look for competitor data."

No business operates in a vacuum. Every transaction in which a company takes part discloses information about the firm's operations—information that may prove vital in competitive analysis. A supplier may know something about a new product design, a customer about production problems, a market research firm about marketing plans, a union representative about labor negotiations.

. . . .

Information Key

Stop right now and think of three areas in which your principal competitor does business. List the important information that might be revealed in these transactions, whether or not you think you can gain access to it.

1. _____

2. _____

3. _____

. . . .

Customers

Your own and your competitors' customers can provide a great deal of information for competitor analysis. Key customers often have detailed information about a competitor's sales levels and pricing strategies. They may also know about new product plans, quality control problems, distribution and delivery systems, sales methods, service level, credit terms, and many other aspects of the business.

For example, Bic Corp. once heard about a scheduled product intro-

Action Probes

What specific information might one of your competitor's customers pass on that you could use to gain a competitive advantage?

Would a poll of competitors' customers uncover dissatisfactions about their products or service that you could exploit?

duction by rival Gillette from one of Gillette's large Canadian customers. Bic speeded up its own product development and was able to reach the market with a similar product almost simultaneously, six months earlier than it had originally planned.

Customers may point directly to a competitor's weaknesses. A chemical company's salespeople found that a major customer was using specialty chemicals rather than the cheaper commodity product it could have substituted for one application because the manufacturer of the commodity chemical took a lax attitude toward delivery and service. This indicated a competitive opening for rivals of the firm.

Another company trained salespeople to conduct rudimentary service on its office products. That enabled them to get past customer purchasing agents and talk to product users and others inside the customer firms with the specific idea of gaining competitor information.

In many cases, even loyal customers of your competitors will be willing to talk freely about their dealings with the rival. They see it in their interest to air complaints and to stimulate competition that might result in better products, lower prices, or improved service. Some techniques for eliciting customer input are:

Have a team of top executives go out and talk with the managers of key customers on a regular basis. Ask: How can we serve you better? In what ways are our competitors failing to meet your needs?

Run industry seminars and conferences in which customers and potential customers are invited to air their views on all industry participants.

Conduct surveys that ask customers to rank the strengths and weaknesses of all the firms in the field—your own and competitors.

Ask one of your solid customers to issue a request for proposals on which a competitor is likely to bid. His proposal may reveal technical and manufacturing capabilities.

Part A of Competitive Analysis Worksheet 9 at the end of the chapter gives you space to fill in the names of competitors' customers that prove to be good sources of information. It's important to keep track of the people inside these companies who are willing to talk about competitor topics.

Some of the questions you might address to customers include:

Why are they satisfied with their current supplier?

What might induce them to switch to another vendor?

What are their principal complaints?

Which firms do they see as the market leaders in your industry?

Which needs are going unfulfilled?

What do they see as the key factors in purchasing decisions?

What changes are approaching in the market?

Suppliers

Suppliers know a great deal about competitors. Usually they are willing to reveal information, especially if they are selling to your company, or hope to be in the future. For example, a supplier's level of delivery of a basic raw material to a competitor may parallel the competitor's sales level.

Don't stop with suppliers of materials and components. Equipment vendors can give you warning of a competitor's upgrading his factory or increasing the automation of his production—possibly with the aim of gaining a cost or capacity advantage.

. . . .

Information Key

A good way to focus on the type of information suppliers might provide you about competitors is to consider what your own suppliers know about your company. Think of three important suppliers of your own and list a valuable piece of information about you that they would be able to provide your competition.

Supplier _____ Information _____

_____

_____

Supplier _____ Information _____

_____

_____

Supplier _____ Information _____

_____

_____

. . . .

Suppliers of labor, such as employment agencies, can give you an idea of changes in work force level. One company entrusted the hiring for a new factory to a single agency. Through this third party, a competitor was able to discover not only the size and makeup of the work force, but the start-up date for the plant. Suppliers of capital, such as banks, may possess advanced knowledge of either expansion plans or financial difficulties. Discreet inquiries can uncover at least some of this data.

Use Part B of Competitive Analysis Worksheet 9 to compile a list of valuable information sources among suppliers. Don't hesitate to use your leverage with these companies if your own firm does business with them as well.

Middlemen

Agents, wholesalers, retailers, distributors, sales reps, and catalog companies often know a great deal about individual firms as well as about the market as a whole. They can give you important feedback on which products are selling and which aren't—and why. They may be able to alert you to unfilled end-user needs.

Middlemen can also inform you of direct competitor moves. For example, a food processing company was alerted by its main distributor that a competitor was about to introduce a new packaging and pricing scheme that could take market share from the company's products. The firm rushed to upgrade its own packaging and to prepare promotions that would blunt the effect of the competitor's action.

When seeking middlemen who can provide information, focus on those who handle a large volume of the competitor's products. Again, keep track of the persons within these companies who are likely to be good sources, with Part C of Competitive Analysis Worksheet 9.

Other Competitors

Form alliances with executives of companies that compete against your major competitors but not directly against your firm. One retailer obtained important information on a chain store that was moving into its geographic territory by checking with another independent retailer that competed against the chain in another part of the country. The two stores' managers exchanged information on how the chain operated and its advertising and merchandising policies.

Other competitors who could provide information are those who compete against a company in a different product area than you do. For example, a company that competes against IBM in minicomputers might find it useful to consult with a firm that competes in disc drives. Both firms could profit from a discussion of topics like IBM's product introduction strategy.

Action Probes

Can you spot weaknesses in competitors' relations with middlemen that might help you to tie up more supply channels and block competitors' access to markets?

Might coordinated efforts with other competitors of your major rivals help both of you to compete more effectively? Would joint ventures prove useful?

. . . .

Use Part D of Competitive Analysis Worksheet 9 to record the names of information sources from among mutual competitors. Be particularly on the lookout for firms whose market share has been eroded or which have been otherwise damaged by your rivals.

Journalists

A reporter writing a story for a newspaper or magazine often collects a great deal more information than he prints. By cooperating with him and developing a quid pro quo relationship, you can turn him into a valuable source of fact and rumor about your competitors and industry. Journalists are almost always willing to talk freely "off the record." If you handle an interview skillfully, you can sometimes gain as much information on competitors as you give out about your own firm.

Remember, though, that the job of every reporter is to print news. Be very careful about how far you go in revealing important company information that you wouldn't want to be generally disclosed. Part E of Competitive Analysis Worksheet 9 gives you room to list information sources among journalists. Make sure the contact person within your company is carefully selected and monitored.

Consultants

Business consultants specializing in your industry will have a great deal of knowledge about the business, much of it obtained through

. . . .

Information Key

Locate an article in a newspaper or magazine that discusses one of your important competitors. Answer the following questions.

1. Who wrote the article? _____
2. How would you rate the quality and currency of the information about the competitor contained in the article?
   __ Excellent   __ Good   __ Fair   __ Poor
3. What other competitor data might the author have uncovered in his research?

   _____

4. How could the author be developed as a potential source of competitor information?

   _____

. . . .

inside examination of competitors' operations. While confidentiality will prevent them from revealing specific facts about companies they've worked with, they can provide you with valuable generalizations about market trends and developments.

Two publications that can help you identify useful consulting organizations are:

Consultants and Consulting Organizations Directory
(8,000 firms and individuals in 135 fields)

International Consultants
(3,000 firms in 100 countries)

both available from: Gale Research Co.
Book Tower
Detroit, MI 48226

Use Part F of Competitive Analysis Worksheet 9 to list useful information sources among consultants. Keep in mind that consultants are in the information business, so that a retainer relationship or frequent contracts for special projects are likely to make the consultant more willing to provide you with desired data.

Unions

Through both informal talks and formal bargaining sessions, you can gain significant competitor information from union representatives. Areas of inquiry might include:

Competitors' wage rates

Work rules

Contract terms

Morale of competitors' workers

Productivity and automation strategies

Work force levels, number of shifts, overtime, absenteeism

Quality control problems

List useful union contacts in Part G of Competitive Analysis Worksheet 9.

Advocacy Groups

These organizations are concerned with areas like:

Environmental and pollution issues

Consumer protection

Product safety

Civil rights

Occupational safety and health

They often conduct extensive research on companies and industries. The information gathered may be of interest to competitors. In addition, the actions of these groups can themselves have competitive implications. For example, continued complaints from safety groups about fire dangers in Ford's Pinto model affected the competitive position of that car.

From a competitor analysis perspective, it is worthwhile for your firm to maintain lines of communication with advocacy groups active in your industry. Informal talks with group officials can often uncover valuable data.

Assign representatives to talk to advocacy groups and show interest in their causes. Keep track of any moves they make that might have competitive consequences. Track these contacts in Part H of Competitive Analysis Worksheet 9.

Analysts and Brokers

Researchers at major stockbroker firms and investment banks follow developments within industries and companies. Because they frequently talk to company executives, they may pick up word of significant plans and developments. Keep in mind, though, that their perspective is always from an investment point of view, not an operating one. This may give rise to opinions and biases that affect their information.

If your major rivals are public companies, it might be useful to cultivate relationships with the securities analysts who follow them. A source that will help you to locate them is the *Directory of Securities Research* (Nelson Publications, 11 Elm Place, Rye, NY 10580), which lists the analysts covering more than 3,000 corporations.

Even if analysts aren't likely to provide information on specific competitors, they conduct research on industries and markets, some of which is available to the public. List sources among analysts whom you find useful in Part I of Competitive Analysis Worksheet 9.

Other Groups

The groups mentioned above are the principal third-party sources of competitor information, but many other potential sources exist. *Anyone* who knows about your competitors should be viewed as a possible source. You need not make efforts to encourage any source to break bonds of confidentiality. But rumors and informal discussions can provide bits of data that can prove to be valuable in completing your view of a competitor's actions.

A good way to tap these sources is to ask them to verify a "rumor." You might say to a real estate developer, "I hear Company X is planning to put in a new plant in the West Side Industrial Park." He may answer, "Yes, I've heard that myself, it's going to be a 200,000-square-feet processing facility." Or he might say, "No, I know there have been no new sales in that development." Or, "I don't know about that, I'll have to look into it." In any case, you've added one more piece of evidence or confirmation to your collection.

Make sure that all your people are aware of the potential value of any information on competitors, no matter what the source. Use Part J of Competitive Analysis Worksheet 9 to keep track of useful sources. Here are some of the types of information you might be able to uncover:

Source	Information
Patent attorneys	Details on patents applied for or granted, patent searches
Advertising agencies	Evaluation of competitor's marketing strength or rumors about his advertising strategy
Real estate developers	Data on land or facility purchases and sales, plant expansion
Accountants	Details of competitor's financial controls or decision-making process
Investment bankers	Advance word of new equity or debt financing, or of merger and acquisition activity

Research Services

Many commercial organizations will sell information or conduct competitor research for a fee. You won't want to use them indiscriminately and they can never take the place of a strong in-house capability. But they may provide important data on an individualized, cost-effective basis.

In some cases, these sources may have access to information that is not available to you. In others, they may have the expertise to gather specific data more quickly, effectively, and thoroughly than you could through your own efforts.

Market Research

Companies have long used market research firms to study markets they are planning to enter, identify viable product ideas, investigate marketing and promotional tactics, and conduct general surveys of market conditions. These firms can also look at the strengths and weaknesses of competitors' products and evaluate specific moves in pricing, packaging, and distribution.

Choose a market research firm that is experienced in your particular industry. The firm's flexibility in meeting your information needs, as well as its skill in communicating data to you, should be prime points in making a selection. The reference work *Directory of U.S. and Canadian Marketing Surveys and Services* (Charles H. Kline & Co., 330 Passaic Ave., Fairfield, NJ 07006) is a good start in looking for the right firm.

Some market research companies put out regular generic reports on specific markets. These can be helpful in supplementing your own research. For example, the Economist Intelligence Unit (Spencer House, 27 St. James Place, London SW1A 1NT, England) makes available numerous studies on topics ranging from paper and packaging, retail, and energy to tourism. Other companies include:

Frost & Sullivan, Inc.

(surveys range from graphic arts supplies to pet products)
106 Fulton St.
New York, NY 10038

A.C. Nielsen Co.

(studies include bimonthly audits of food, health, and beauty goods)
Nielsen Plaza
Northbrook, IL 60062

Stanford Research Institute

(in-depth reports on the chemical and hydrocarbon markets with regular updates)
333 Ravenswood Ave.
Menlo Park, CA 94025

Credit Agencies

These firms sell financial data on companies from a creditworthiness perspective. Some of the information can be useful in competitor analysis, especially in the case of private firms where no other financial data is available.

Interestingly, the background information on a company's owners, which is often included with the credit report, can sometimes be more useful than the financial facts. The background and business experience of a competitor's principals can give a good indication of how they will act in the future.

Two leading sources of credit information are:

Dun & Bradstreet, Inc.

99 Church Street
New York, NY 10007

TRW Information Services Division
505 City Parkway West
Orange, CA 92668

Information Specialists

There are a growing number of companies that conduct customized research on competitors or industries for their clients. These firms will provide a full report or can tailor the research to uncovering a very specific fact.

For example, Perrier USA contracted with such a company to conduct a study of the U.S. bottled water market, including data on competition, prices, and trends. The information aided the company's very successful entry into the market. The Hospital Products Division of Abbott Laboratories uses such research firms to spot promising product areas, in which it then conducts in-depth market research itself.

An information search conducted by a specialist like Information Data Search (80 Trowbridge Street, Cambridge, MA 02138) would contain such categories as industry, problem, background, intelligence gathered for client, client action, and sales (market breakout, customers contacted, findings, further details).

These are a good illustration of the type of specific and time-sensitive data that research service firms can help you with. IDS also offers seminars that cover the techniques of competitor information gathering.

Some other companies currently participating in this growing field are:

Arthur D. Little & Co.
25 Acorn Pk.
Cambridge, MA 02140

Barker and Associates
2936 Domingo St.
Berkeley, CA 94705

Business International Corp.

1 Dag Hammarskjöld Plaza
New York, NY 10017

Find/SVP

500 Fifth Ave.
New York, NY 10010

International Data Corp.

5 Speen Street
Framingham, MA 01701

Predicasts, Inc.

11001 Cedar Ave.
Cleveland, Ohio 44106

Washington Researchers, Ltd.

918 16th St., N.W.
Washington, DC 20006

World Wide Information Service, Inc.

660 First Ave.
New York, NY 10016

COMPETITIVE ANALYSIS WORKSHEET 9

THIRD-PARTY INFORMATION SOURCES: CHECKLIST

A. Customers

Company	Our Customer (Yes/No)	Customer of (Competitor)	Useful Contact	Type of Information
_____	_____	_____	_____	_____
_____	_____	_____	_____	_____
_____	_____	_____	_____	_____

B. Suppliers

Company	Our Supplier (Yes/No)	Serves (Competitor)	Useful Contact	Type of Information
_____	_____	_____	_____	_____
_____	_____	_____	_____	_____
_____	_____	_____	_____	_____

C. Middlemen

Company	Functions as (e.g., Wholesaler)	Serves (Competitor)	Useful Contact	Type of Information
_____	_____	_____	_____	_____
_____	_____	_____	_____	_____
_____	_____	_____	_____	_____

D. Other Competitors

Company	Competes with (Competitor)	Market Area of Competition	Useful Contact	Type of Information
___	___	___	___	___
___	___	___	___	___
___	___	___	___	___

E. Journalist

Name	Publication	Contact in Our Company	Type of Information
___	___	___	___
___	___	___	___

F. Consultants

Name	Company	Contact in Our Company	Type of Information
___	___	___	___
___	___	___	___

G. Unions

Representative	Union	Represents Workers at (Competitor)	Type of Information
___	___	___	___
___	___	___	___

H. Advocacy Groups

Group	General Concern	Contact in Group	Specific Action Related to Competitors
_____	_____	_____	_____
_____	_____	_____	_____

I. Securities Analysts

Name	Firm	Competitor(s) Followed	Type of Information
_____	_____	_____	_____
_____	_____	_____	_____

J. Other Sources

Name	Firm	Knowledge about (Competitors)	Type of Information
_____	_____	_____	_____
_____	_____	_____	_____

9

Organizing and Communicating Competitive Information

The goal of your competitor analysis program is to gain insights into how competitors act and react. An accumulation of data is worthless if it does not supply you with this meaning. The main value of competitor information lies in the action that your company takes.

Your first step in transforming raw data into action is to organize it properly and make it accessible in an efficient and timely manner to decision makers in various parts of your company.

The Right Amount

Begin by collecting the right amount of information. An excess of data has two negative effects on typical managers:

It discourages them from considering competitor factors at all. File folders bulging with undigested facts are unlikely to be read by busy managers who need to make immediate decisions.

It mires them in details. They see only isolated facts and are unable to view larger patterns and trends.

The best way to avoid this information overload is to ask of each bit of data: "How does it pertain to the future?" For example, does it indicate a mistake the competitor is likely to repeat? Does it show that the rival has gained market share and that appropriate defensive actions are required? As one expert in the field contends, competitive analysis is not to record the past or even describe the present, but to prepare for the future.

Figure 6 is an example of how competitive analysis is used as a weapon in the business wars.

Procedures for Organization and Dissemination

As with every aspect of competitive analysis, the way you handle the information you've collected depends to a great extent on your com-

. . . .

Information Key

Think of two competitor actions in the past that created problems for your company. In what ways could competitive analysis have given you the information in advance that would have helped you to deal with the difficulties?

Situation 1: _____

_____

Situation 2: _____

_____

. . . .

pany and the individual needs of information users. Modify the following seven-step plan to suit your own situation.

Step 1: Evaluate the Data

Each piece of data—statistics drawn from a reference work, rumors passed on by a salesperson, estimates from a magazine article—should be judged according to reliability and accuracy. Reliability refers to the source of the information: To what extent has the source provided accurate information in the past? Accuracy refers to the piece of information itself: Is it true or not? Remember that reliable sources can occasionally yield inaccurate information, just as an unreliable source can give you accurate data from time to time.

Reliability judgments result from your record of experience with the source, as well as from your estimation of the source's bias or vested interest in the data. A securities analyst, for example, may prove to be a highly reliable source of industry gossip. On the other hand, one of your salespeople may make a habit of forwarding speculative and self-serving information.

Accuracy must ultimately rest on corroboration. If two independent sources agree, the information is likely to be true. If they disagree,

---

PRINCIPLES OF ORGANIZATION AND DISSEMINATION

According to a U.S. Army Field Manual entitled *Combat Intelligence,* "The degree of success achieved by any unit in accomplishing its mission will be directly affected by the intelligence which it develops and uses, and the manner in which it is used." In many ways, competitive information should be handled in the same way as military intelligence.

The following principles for handling intelligence are condensed from another Army manual, *Operations.* Their application to competitor analysis is clear.

1. Evaluate the information.
    a. Is it pertinent to present events?
    b. Is it urgent?
    c. Is it accurate
        1) Has it been corroborated by previous information?
        2) Does it agree or disagree with what is known?
        3) If it does not agree, which information is more likely to be true?
2. Interpret the information.
    a. What is its meaning in connection with currently known facts?
    b. Does it alter or add to the perceptions of the situation?
    c. Does it confirm other information?
    d. What is its significance in relation to current goals?
3. Disseminate the information on a timely basis.
    a. By means of summaries
    b. Through operational orders
    c. At briefings and conferences
    d. Through incorporation into situation reports

Figure 6. Competitive Analysis as a Weapon in the Business Wars

one may be true, or both may be wrong. When you make an estimate of accuracy in the absence of corroboration, the reliability of the source and judgment based on experience are your guides.

Competitive Analysis Worksheet 10 at the end of this chapter gives you a form for recording information before filing it. Reproduce this form and distribute it to departmental liaisons and others who will work with the competitive intelligence group in gathering data. Small bits of data can be recorded in full on the sheet, or you can attach it as a cover sheet to reports, articles, or documents.

Step 2: Establish the Base Files

These files—best arranged in looseleaf notebooks—should contain profiles of principal competitors as well as additional data on selected key factors. The basic information will be compiled in the Competitive Analysis Worksheets you'll find in Chapters 11, 12, and 13 for each competitor. Together, these sheets will give you a general overview of each company, along with an analysis of its strengths and weaknesses, in a form readily accessible to decision makers. Pertinent supplementary documents can be included as well.

Some points to keep in mind about your base files:

Update them regularly.

Use them to summarize competitor data in other files.

Keep them simple. Don't burden them with unnecessary documents.

Seek feedback on the accuracy and relevance of information in the files from end-users.

Step 3: Establish a Filing and Indexing System

The competitor landscape with which you are dealing will dictate the form of your filing and indexing system. "For a firm with a small number of competitors," explains Information Data Search president Leonard Fuld, "a simple system filed according to competitors is sufficient. For a firm like ITT, a system that organizes data according to industry group or market would be needed."

A simple way to set up your filing system is to file it alphabetically according to key words. This system groups information according to both topic and company. It simplifies filing and produces an orderly arrangement. An index with extensive cross-references provides access to all data. Such an index is briefly illustrated in Figure 7.

Many companies today are turning to microcomputers to facilitate keeping track of competitor information. Simple programs allow you to

. . . .

Information Key

If you currently maintain files on competitors, review them and ask your-self: "Could a busy line manager faced with a pressing decision obtain a clear picture of a competitor from a quick glance at these files?" If not, in what ways could they be improved?

_____

_____

_____

_____

. . . .

A SAMPLE KEY—WORD INDEX

Words in CAPITALS indicate a particular file or heading. Lower case words are cross-referenced. Letters and numbers indicate the location of the data in the filing system.

CTS CORP—[C1])
	see also:	ENGINE SENSORS [E8]
		SWITCHES [S26]
		AUTO COMPONENTS (ELECTRONICS) [A17]

California
| | see: | ENVIRONMENTAL REGULATION [E11] |
| | | SALES (WESTERN REGION) [S4] |

CANADA—[C2]
| | see also: | EXPORTS TRADE [E26] |
| | | TARIFFS [T5] |

Carbonization
| | see: | MAINTENANCE [M10] |
| | | VALVES [V4] |

CARBURETORS—[C3]
| | see also: | ROCHESTER PRODUCTS [R14] |
| | | TESTING PROCEDURES [T13] |

Figure 7. *A Brief Example of a Word Index*

continually update references. Storing the entries in the computer's memory is more convenient than compiling a printed index. Make sure, if you use a computerized system, that it is simple enough to be used by any of your managers seeking access to the information.

Step 4: Set Up an Alert System

A military intelligence system must have a way of distinguishing between reports that indicate "the enemy is building a new supply bunker" and other reports that indicate "an enemy attack is imminent." In the same way, a competitive analysis director should take steps to ensure that his staff does not become so involved in stockpiling data that it misses clear warning signals that competitors are engaged in significant moves.

A building supply concern, Company A, routinely gathered information about a competitor, Company B, which did not then sell construction products in Company A's market area. An alert researcher one day came to the competitive analysis director and pointed out that in the past month Company B had hired two former salespeople from Company C, a rival who possessed a large share of the local market.

Did this mean that Company B was considering an attempt to penetrate the market? Was the firm specifically seeking personnel with local knowledge?

Further investigation verified this theory. Company B had even approached some of Company A's own salespeople. It had hired a market research firm to study local conditions and had approached a realtor in the area to look for a warehouse site.

Set up a system to draw attention to key competitive factors. Competitive Analysis Worksheet 10, at the end of the chapter, includes a priority rating for classifying the urgency of the data. This is a first step. You should also set up specific criteria indicating that the competitor information must be given detailed attention. These criteria will depend on the competitive climate you face. Some possibilities:

A competitor's market share increases by more than two percent in a quarter.

An executive is hired from outside the firm at the vice-president level or higher.

The competitor adds more than 10 percent to its labor force during a specific month.

The competitor takes on a bank loan or line of credit greater than five percent of current capitalization.

The competitor introduces an across-the-board price cut or lowers prices more than 10 percent on a key product.

Step 5: Review and Evaluate Information Sources

Establish procedures to periodically review all sources of competitor information. This exercise serves several purposes:

1. It eliminates your wasting time consulting useless sources. If a particular periodical, report, or trade show never yields useful competitor data, you need not spend time on it in the future.

2. It focuses your attention on the most useful sources. When you see that much of your most valuable information has come from one source—a trade journal or one of the competitor's customers—you can intensify your use of it.

3. It pushes you to seek new sources. Your review will point out to you which sources are not contributing any information. For example, maybe your purchasing department has not passed along data from competitors' suppliers despite the fact that several competitors have switched materials. Your review should prompt you to increase competitive awareness in this area and to stimulate the flow of information.

Competitive Analysis Worksheet 11 at the end of this chapter gives you a checklist to review individual information sources. You can modify it to fit particular types of sources—government, published, trade, personal contacts—and to take into account your own information needs. Fill out one such form for every potential source of data.

. . . .

Action Probes

How could early warning signs allow you to counter a specific competitor tactic such as a price cut?

What actions could you take to send false signals to competitors before one of your own moves?

. . . .

Step 6: Weed the Files

This step should be an ongoing, integral part of your organizational procedures. Establish a schedule to sort through every file regularly and eliminate all material no longer useful. Otherwise, the files will expand to an extent that current, useful data will become buried in a mountain of trivia and dated facts.

Most companies set up a schedule for discarding data. For example, you might retain competitors' annual reports for five years, quarterly reports for one year, sales forecasts for six months, capital spending information for three years, and so forth.

An ongoing procedure which ensures that each file is reviewed each year would consist of:

1. A staff member examines the file and removes any data which appears dated or irrelevant.

2. Another staff member, or the competitive analysis director, examines the material that has been removed to make sure it contains nothing of value.

3. Data that may be of historical interest (e.g., for establishing long-term trends) is transferred to inactive files. The remainder of the material is destroyed.

Step 7: Set Up a Dissemination System

Just as important as collecting useful information is communicating facts and analyses to decision makers. Several means of doing this are available.

Situation Reports

These give an overview of general developments concerning a competitor or group of competitors. They may result from a quarterly review of the competitor base file by the competitive analysis director, and should be distributed to a wide range of managers.

They may also be prepared in order to answer the needs of managers and committees working on budgets, strategic plans, marketing strategies, or new products. The marketing department, for example, may wish to take a broad look at several competitors before deciding how much to allocate to advertising and promotions for the coming year. In these cases, the situation report would focus on particular areas and be forwarded to the interested party.

Some companies circulate a competitor newsletter. This is the equivalent of an ongoing situation report. It keeps managers up-to-date on competitor developments and also increases their competitive awareness.

Special Reports

Information that has come to the attention of the competitive analysis staff may be briefly summarized in a special report. Such a report might discuss a competitor's new pricing structure, a management change that is likely to result in new tactics, or it may analyze possible competitor reactions to new technological developments in the market.

These reports should be as brief as possible, backed up with facts, and distributed to all managers affected. Figure 8 gives a hypothetical illustration of a typical special report.

Tactical Reports

Communication about competitive analysis is a two-way street. Operating managers frequently want to know details of competitor activities or plans in order to guide their own decisions. When making these requests for tactical information, they should be as specific as possible. The following examples illustrate the difference between general and specific questions:

General	Specific
What are Ajax Co.'s product plans?	Does Ajax Co. have plans to upgrade relay T-458?
What is the status of Onyx Corp.'s financial situation?	We've heard that Onyx Corp. is considering extending credit terms to 60 days. Do they have the working capital resources to do so?
How capable is Pyramid Co.'s management?	Pyramid Co. is moving into direct sales for the first time. How experienced is their new sales manager in this area?

SPECIAL COMPETITOR REPORT

SUBJECT: Dynax Company—new product development
DATE: October 10, 19xx
PRIORITY: Routine
ATTENTION: Sales, Marketing, Engineering, Customer Service

We expect Dynax to announce within the next six weeks an addition to its high-speed communications switching line. The exact specifications of the new device are not yet known. It is expected to be an improvement on their Dynaleco model F 1104-R.

The move represents a further attempt to capture the medium-range OEM modem market. First deliveries are projected for February.

Refer to competitor files:

[D14]—speech by Dynax president L. Wilson at the August Communications Equipment Association Conference

[D17]—information from purchasing manager at Argon Corporation (Dynax customer)

[S18]—Communications News article (9/28) discussing modem switch market.

Figure 8. A Hypothetical Special Competitive Report

REQUEST FOR COMPETITOR INFORMATION

Requested by _____ Date _____

Department _____ Title _____

General Topic: _____

Competitor concerned (if any): _____

Information need is: URGENT _____ Important _____ Routine _____

Needed by (date): _____

Likely source of information: _____

Describe the information needed briefly but in detail (be specific):

_____

_____
_____

Figure 9. Request for Competitor Information

Requests for information should be clear and avoid jargon, overly technical language, and ambiguity. They should recommend possible sources of information, for example, "Company A is a big user of this relay; check with its purchasing people." An idea of the urgency and importance of the requested information should also be conveyed. Figure 9 shows a request form used by one company. You can adapt it and make copies for your managers who may be seeking tactical competitor information.

The tactical reports that reply to these requests should take the same form as special reports. Each should be formulated as a specific answer to the question raised, not as a general discussion of the topic. If the information cannot be found, the report should state so, give any related data that has been uncovered, and ask for recommendations about alternative information sources.

Competitor Briefing Meetings

Use these meetings to inform a group of managers about important competitor developments. They are particularly useful when the development calls for an immediate response on the part of your company—the entry into the market of a powerful new competitor, a competitor's drastic price reduction on an important product, a technological breakthrough, and so forth.

The competitive analysis director should summarize the pertinent data and clearly outline the choices and decisions that it imposes on the company. He should be ready to support his views with data and back up his presentation with a written report and thorough documentation.

COMPETITIVE ANALYSIS WORKSHEET 10

COMPETITOR INFORMATION REPORT FORM

Filed by _____ Date _____

Department _____ Title _____

Source of Information _____

General Topic _____

Information is: Competitor-specific ____ Industry-general ____

Product discussed (if any) _____

Priority: Urgent ____ Important ____ Routine ____

Reliability of Source	(circle)		Accuracy of Information
Almost always reliable	3	3	Corroborated
Usually reliable	2	2	Very likely accurate
Often reliable	1	1	Probably accurate
Sometimes reliable	0	0	Can't judge accuracy
Often unreliable	-1	-1	Probably inaccurate
Frequently unreliable	-2	-2	Very likely inaccurate
Almost always unreliable	-3	-3	Definitely inaccurate

Give a clear, brief account of information:

_____

_____

_____

_____

_____

Documents attached? Yes ____ No ____

COMPETITIVE ANALYSIS WORKSHEET 11

INFORMATION SOURCE REVIEW FORM

Reviewed by _____ Date _____

Department _____ Title _____

Source _____

Type of source:

_____ In-house department/person

_____ Competitor contact

_____ Third party; specify: _____

_____ Reference work

_____ Periodical

_____ Government publication

_____ Personal contact

_____ Interview with: _____

Period of time covered by review: _____

How often source used during period: _____

How often used successfully: _____

Quality of information:

_____ Vital   _____ Routine   _____ Mixed

_____ Important   _____ Marginal

Uniqueness of useful material:

_____ Not available elsewhere

_____ Available but not widely known

_____ Widely available

Accuracy of information provided:

    Number of references that proved accurate ____

    Number of references that proved inaccurate ____

    Number of references for which accuracy not established ____

Overall rating of source:

    ____ Very useful   ____ Occasionally useful

    ____ Sometimes useful   ____ Never useful

Comments:

_____

_____

_____

_____

_____

_____

10

Developing a Framework for Your Competitive Analysis Program

Before you begin a detailed analysis of individual competitors, you should take a look at the parameters of your market, the current and potential competitors you most need to examine, and the ways in which you can spot competitive strengths and weaknesses—your own and those of rival firms.

Market Analysis

Competitive Analysis Worksheet 12 gives you a form that, when filled in, will provide you with a concise overview of your market. Its information should be the first priority of your data collection efforts. Some numbers will need to be estimated. Reproduce the form and complete it for each distinct market segment in which you participate.

Concentration

Part A of Worksheet 12 gives you a picture of the concentration in your market—the shares controlled by leading participants. If you do not have exact data, try to make an educated guess as to a competitor's market share in order to establish a pattern.

The number of firms participating in a market and the distribution of market share are important factors in the dynamics of competition. For example, in a highly concentrated industry, the few participants may recognize their interdependence and minimize competitive pressures on each other; international airlines, cigarette companies, and petroleum producers are all relatively concentrated industries where competition has been restrained by actual or tacit agreements. On the other hand, a strong competitive battle can break out in a concentrated market with severe consequences to some participants. When Procter & Gamble's Citrus Hill brand began competing with Beatrice's Tropicana in the fresh orange juice market, the struggle between these market powers had devastating effects on smaller processors and house brands.

Fragmented industries are usually characterized by mild competition as each participant serves a well-defined niche. Printers, for example, often specialize in particular areas of service within a well-defined geographic area. Competition is restrained. However, a competitor may attempt to overcome fragmentation, rearranging the competitive climate faced by local firms.

Both market share and total concentration patterns for the industry are important points to study as you conduct competitor analysis. To begin with, market share has been shown to be directly related to return on investment (ROI)—high market share translates into high return. A study by the Strategic Planning Institute found that companies with over 36 percent market share averaged 30.2 percent ROI, versus 9.6 percent ROI for firms with less than seven percent share.

The larger effect of industry concentration can be seen in the following examples.

1. The breakfast food industry is highly concentrated, with the top four companies in the U.S. accounting for 90 percent of sales. Competition in price has traditionally been restrained (a number of large producers, in fact, were investigated for antitrust violations during the 1970s).

Only 52 percent of the selling price of cereals, on average, is taken up by material and direct labor costs. The remaining 48 percent is available for research, overhead, and especially marketing. Advertising expenditures are enormous, but they represent more a formidable obstacle to new entrants than they do a direct struggle among current participants.

2. Beer production has become increasingly concentrated, with the number of independent companies in the industry dropping from 150 in 1963 to 40 in 1985. Market share of the five largest firms increased from 40 percent to 75 percent during that period.

Marketing wars among the top participants, with heavy use of television advertising, have created a competitive climate in which smaller breweries have a tough time competing. Many have been taken over by the giants.

3. The restaurant business has traditionally been a fragmented one, with local operators serving local tastes and needs. McDonald's was able to overcome the fragmentation by creating economies of scale in production and marketing. Individual restaurants, as well as regional chains, soon found themselves facing a far different competitive situation.

Segmenting Your Markets

The many ways in which a particular industry can be divided play a role in everything from market definition to competitive strategy. Consider the ways in which your major markets are segmented. Which competitors are the leaders in particular segments? Do competitors segment the market in a different way than you do? For example, do they sell one product line through mail order, another through retailers (distribution segmentation), while you sell several different models through both direct mail and retail (product segmentation)?

Consider just a few of the many ways that a market can be segmented.

1. Material has become an important segment element in the apparel industry, with natural fiber fabrics (cotton, wool) and synthetics defining specific market segments.

2. Distribution channels can determine market segments. The book industry divides products into trade books (sold through book stores) and mass market books (sold through general retail outlets).

The toy market in Germany is divided into the following distribution segments:

Specialty toy stores	42%
Department stores	33%
Hypermarkets	15%
Mail order	5%
Other	5%

Information Key

Is your principal market concentrated or fragmented? Jot down several ways in which this alignment affects competition in that market.

_____

_____

_____

_____

. . . .

3. Product type is naturally an important segmentation category. For example, the bicycle market in Germany is divided into the following model categories:

Sports	30%
Racer/sports	21%
BMX	17%
Youth	16%
Youth/racer	3%
Collapsible	2%
Touring	2%
Racing	1%

4. Incidental aspects of products can define segments. For example, in the U.S. cigarette market, size categories have been important characteristics of segments. Each company offers products in the major size segments: regular, king size, and 100 mm. The Benson and Hedges brand was able to gain a competitive advantage when it successfully pioneered the 100 mm size.

Segmentation is an important consideration in how you analyze your competitors. The way in which a company defines market segments, and the segments that it seeks to serve or that it ignores, will to a great extent define its competitive strategy. For example, People Express has attempted to compete by serving a well-defined market segment: low-priced, "no frills" flights. Concentration on this segment—rather than trying, for example, to attract the more profitable business customer—has allowed the company to quickly build up the volume needed to cover its costs.

Coca-Cola, to take another example, turned its Diet Coke product into the third-largest—selling soft drink by focusing on a segment defined by product ingredient—artificial versus natural sweetener.

The U.S. automobile market was for many years strictly segmented according to price points and model features. Imports broke up these segments by aiming their marketing efforts toward different segments. Specialty producers like Volkswagen were able to tap segments that the big Detroit producers hadn't been aware of.

Part B of Competitive Analysis Worksheet 12 directs you in defining the principal segments in your markets. This definition will depend on your judgment and your evaluation of the forces affecting the market. Make sure that the segments you define really represent the *most fundamental* definition of the market sectors.

For example, the wine market is clearly segmented according to different types and prices of wine. But the true basis of segmentation from the wine marketers' perspective is customer groups. Vintage wine drinkers have different tastes than purchasers of mass-produced wines and each will choose different products regardless of price.

Below is a list of some of the ways in which a market can be segmented. There are many others. Consider all possible ones when thinking about your own markets.

Product Segments
Price
Quality
Durability
Materials
Construction
Model or brand name

Distribution Segments

Direct sales

Original equipment manufacturers

Wholesalers

Retailers

Jobbers, agents

Lease versus buy

Customer Segments

Product use

Frequency of buying

Volume of purchase

Demographics (age, sex, income, etc.)

Industry

Desegmentation: Another Route

Good segment definition and target marketing are accepted paths to success. This has been the case in the brewing industry as it has elsewhere. But Stroh Brewing Co. tried a different tack with its Old Milwaukee brand.

Old Milwaukee was acquired by Stroh when that company took over the ailing Schlitz brands. Old Milwaukee fit squarely into the low-end segment of a market that is divided according to price points (low-priced, premium, super-premium, and imports).

What Stroh attempted to do in its marketing, though, was to blur the distinction between low-priced and premium beers. It used heavy, consistent national advertising to promote Old Milwaukee as a popular-priced, high-quality product. The idea was to gain market share in both the low-priced and premium segments.

The risk that you take with desegmentation is that your product will fall between two segments and fail to appeal to either. But marketing in-

. . . .

Information Key

Once you have defined as accurately as possible the way your market is currently segmented, ask yourself: What new segments are possible? Could you target these segments through product or marketing changes? List two potential segments and judge their viability.

_____

_____

_____

_____

. . . .

novation sometimes succeeds if properly planned and executed. This seems to be the case with Old Milwaukee, as the brand's sales grew by 16.3 percent in 1983 while total beer sales inched forward by only 1.5 percent.

Growth Factors

The rate of growth of a market—and each of its segments—exerts considerable influence on competitive analysis and strategy. Consider the common characteristics of two extremes of growth:

Emerging Industries	Declining Industries
Customer uncertainty	Competition for market share
Heavy investment requirements	Experienced buyers
Rapidly declining costs	Technological stability

Entry by many new competitors	Increased segmentation
Technological volatility	Lower investment requirements
Industry shakeouts	High profitability for market leader

Part C of Competitive Analysis Worksheet 12 lets you estimate the growth in your own markets. Be sure to look at real growth—in units or weighted currency—as opposed to the illusory growth created by inflation.

Geographic Factors

One special form of segmentation is by geography. The geographic range of competition is an important consideration in deciding who your competitors are. While local or domestic rivals may loom largest, you need to keep your eyes peeled for invaders from afar. Begin by classifying your market by type.

1. Local markets may involve perishable products or may be sensitive to transportation economics. Fresh fish and newspapers are examples of the former, while laundries and the ready-mix concrete industry illustrate the latter.

2. Regional markets may require that the producer be attuned to area needs and preferences, or may result from economies of scale that outweigh factors that would otherwise limit the business to local markets. Poultry processors, for example, have economies that allow them to ship their perishable products beyond local market borders. Retail chains are often regional, as are many service firms such as industrial security companies and employment agencies.

3. Domestic markets are nationwide but don't cross international borders. Trade restrictions or local conditions may determine this alignment. Insurance is usually a domestic industry, as are appliances and processed foods (tastes differ from one country to another).

. . . .

Information Key

One competitive tactic is to move quickly into a rapidly growing market segment. For example, in the restaurant industry, the breakfast market increased 57 percent over a recent five-year period. The Burger King chain concentrated on gaining a larger portion of this growth segment, as did specialty restaurants like Le Peep, which serves only breakfasts. Consider the segment of your market that's likely to grow the fastest in the next five years. What are your plans to participate?

Segment: _____

Plans: _____

_____

. . . .

4. International markets exist in areas like commodity products (chemicals, basic steel), many industrial items, and an increasing number of standardized consumer goods. Petroleum, grain, machine tools, and more recently cameras and automobiles all compete in international markets.

Asking the Right Questions

Competitive analysis requires you to ask four questions about the geography of your market:

1. What are the current geographic boundaries of this market?
2. Why is this market limited geographically?
3. What advantages do competitors have as a result of their geographic market coverage?
4. How could the geographic alignment change?

This last question is important. Steel was considered a domestic industry in the United States for many years. Imports in 1960 accounted for only 4.7 percent of the market. But a combination of factors relating to plant modernization, labor costs, and government subsidies allowed the Japanese and European steel producers to grab more than 16 percent of the market by 1980.

Local competitors are often oblivious to developing competitive threats. Real estate sales were always seen as a local business because of the value of personal contacts and facilities in the market area. But organizations like Century 21 and Coldwell Banker have been able to establish nationwide businesses and have competed very effectively with local realtors. One of the reasons: Mobile customers now extend their search for a home over a 40 to 50 mile radius, an area better covered by a group of connected offices than by a single operation.

Likewise, both Dow Jones' *Wall Street Journal* and Gannett's *USA Today* have shown that a daily newspaper can survive in a national market. Local and regional publications have had to adjust to this new competition.

Fill in Part D of Competitive Analysis Worksheet 12, which defines the geographic extent and limitations of your markets. Be careful to look for the reasons why the market is so aligned and for potential changes.

Who Are Your Competitors?

Don't take the definition of who your competitors are for granted. Too many companies define their competition too narrowly. Always consider three classes of competitors:

Current market participants

Potential market entrants

Providers of substitute products

Current Participants

Current participants can be classified as either specialists or generalists. To a large extent, this classification is relative: Are the companies

....

Action Probes

How can you exploit a competitor's location or the location of his market in order to gain a competitive advantage (e.g., by offering free delivery within an important part of the market)?

In what ways might you extend the geographic boundaries of your own markets in order to expand your customer base?

....

more or less specialized than your own? A generalist firm doesn't necessarily participate in a range of unrelated businesses. Rather, it sells in a broader range of markets or market segments than your own. For example, if you produce electrical switches you would see another switch company as a specialist. But you would regard a full-line maker of electrical components as a generalist.

These classifications are an important way of grouping current market participants because they tell a great deal about competitive strategies and thinking. Specialists, for example, are usually more committed to a market or segment than a diversified firm and have more expertise in the area. This influences the way such firms compete. Automobile companies have become increasingly specialized. General Motors, for instance, has eliminated such nonauto businesses as its Frigidaire appliance division. These companies are highly committed to the automobile business and are willing to lose millions of dollars rather than give in to competitors. Forest products companies, tool makers, and mining firms all tend to operate as specialists.

Generalists have other competitive advantages. They may be able to spread economies of scale over a number of business areas. They may make synergistic use of research. Their areas of operation may be countercyclical. Because they are less committed to any one business or segment, they might have greater flexibility in transferring assets or responding to changing markets. Their businesses may be complementary, with a mature, cash-producing unit providing investment funds for an emerging industry.

Generalists can also encounter problems. While firms like General Electric, Westinghouse, Phillips, and Hitachi have been successful in a variety of markets, conglomerates such as ITT and LTV have found diversity more difficult to manage.

Part A of Competitive Analysis Worksheet 13 enables you to list your current competitors and classify each one as a specialist or generalist. Update this list as competitors enter and leave the market.

Potential Competitors

Potential competitors are those companies that could enter your markets in the future. You should look for them in four directions.

1. Geographic Expansion. A manufacturer from another part of the country that previously hadn't sold products in your area contracts with a local distributor to carry his goods. Suddenly you have a new competitor. A foreign company, looking for a new market, begins a major exporting campaign to your home country. You've already examined some of the geographic aspects of your market. Refer to Part D of Competitive Analysis Worksheet 12, then fill in Part B1 of Competitive Analysis Worksheet 13. While you won't be able to carry out a full analysis yet of all of these potential competitors, you can ask:

Which companies in your industry have been expanding geographically?

What attractions does your local market have (e.g., rapid growth) that might encourage a competitor to enter?

What changes have made entry easier (e.g., removal of tariff restrictions)?

2. Forward Integration. In the late 1960s, Perdue Farms, a Maryland producer of live poultry, went into the poultry processing business. The reason: The poultry business was sluggish at the time and company owner Frank Perdue sought to gain the higher margins available in processing. The company's success as an integrated producer, processor, and marketer put pressure on processors who did not have the same control of sources and economies of scale.

Suppliers often adopt forward integration in order to take advantage of the higher margins "downstream." Petroleum producers entered the chemical business for this reason. And steel companies have tried to move into fabricated products.

While companies that integrate forward can rely on a sure source of supply, they often run into production or marketing problems in the business they enter. Texas Instruments, successful in selling semi-conductor components, failed in its attempts to integrate forward into watches and computers.

Use Part B2 of Competitive Analysis Worksheet 13 to track suppliers in your industry who may become competitors through forward integration. Be particularly aware of this threat during times when low prices cut profits for suppliers of materials or components.

3. Backward Integration. More common than forward integration is for producers to enter into competition with suppliers. General Motors originally purchased the majority of the components in its automobiles. Over the years it began to manufacture a greater portion of each car. Auto parts producers experienced a significant competitive impact, especially as GM made parts not only for its own use, but also for the market at large.

One reason DuPont purchased Conoco was to assure supplies of feedstocks for its chemical business. The A&P supermarket chain went into the business of processing and canning food products in order to offer profitable house brands. In the 1960s, Black & Decker began making its own motors to power hand tools. More recently Whirlpool started to produce controls for its appliances rather than purchase them from suppliers.

Part B3 of Competitive Analysis Worksheet 13 asks you to list companies that are currently customers in your industry but that could turn into competitors. Identify them by asking whether these firms could obtain greater security of supply through backward integration. Could they gain more control over their operations? Could they achieve economies?

4. Horizontal Moves. New competitors can also arise from industries closely related to your own. Black & Decker, a successful marketer of hand tools, moved into the small appliance market. Affinities exist

··

Information Key

Imagine that a major customer decided to fully integrate backward. How would this move affect your firm? How would it affect your entire industry?

Your company: _____

_____

Your industry: _____

_____

··

between the two product areas in terms of production, research, and marketing.

Midas, a long-established chain of muffler service shops, broadened its offerings to include brakes and related vehicle maintenance services.

Wang Laboratories, which specialized in word processing, found itself competing with new companies as computer firms like IBM and communications specialists like AT&T moved into the office automation market.

Hospital Corp. of America, in addition to integrating backward through the purchase of American Hospital Supply, moved sideways into nursing homes, medical equipment leasing, and health care insurance. These moves put pressure on direct competitors like Humana as well as on companies in those subsidiary businesses.

Horizontal moves can be difficult to detect in advance. They require you to keep an eye on the management philosophy and strategic direction of many companies in businesses related to yours. What might attract them to your market? How would they benefit by entering it? What advantages do they have to compete against firms currently in the field? List any potential entrants that you can identify in Part B4 of Competitive Analysis Worksheet 13.

Figure 10 provides you with a *Competitor Map* on which you can consolidate the competitors and potential competitors that you face. List them in the order in which you view the competitive threat that they pose, the most important ones first. Keep updating this map as the alignment of competitors facing you changes.

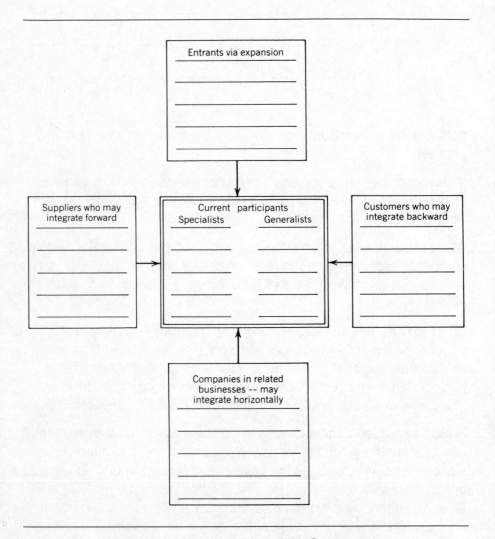

Figure 10. Creating a Map of the Competition

· ·

Action Probes

In what ways could you expand your competitive power outside your current markets (e.g., by integrating backward or adapting your product so that it could take the place of another product with which it currently doesn't compete)?

How could you use sideways integration to offer a more attractive range of products or services than your direct competitors?

· ·

Providers of Substitute Products

Providers of substitute products were discussed in Chapter 3. Generally you will need to conduct an analysis of these companies only when, as a group, they begin to pose a significant threat to your industry. Part C of Competitive Analysis Worksheet 13 gives you space to list any potential substitutes to your products and to rank the threat posed by each.

The Competitive Advantage

Having examined your market and competitors, you should now try to pin down the characteristics that separate winners from losers in your industry. These will become important focal points for further competitive analysis.

Competitive advantages are related to the key factors that you already examined in Chapter 3. They differ in that they represent actual ways in which competitors gain or retain market share. For example, product reliability may be a key factor in your industry, but if all competitors' products are equally reliable, none will gain a competitive advantage. Figure 11 illustrates how one company established a competitive advantage.

Below is a list of 15 of the most important and common competitive advantages. While this is not a definitive list—innumerable advan-

Film processing is a slow-growth, highly competitive field. Key factors, from the customer's point of view, are the speed with which photos are returned and price. It is difficult for a company to obtain a competitive advantage strictly on the basis of speed and price, though, since any competitor can match another in these factors.

Berkey Film Processing, which has competed successfully in this market for many years, began to focus on its competitive advantage by analyzing its market and competitors. Berkey managers noted that 62 percent of film processing sales were conducted through supermarkets, discount stores, and drug store chains. It therefore based its advantage on two tactics:

1. *Customer service:* Viewing the retail outlet as the customer, Berkey helps the store sell more film processing by conducting consumer research, by designing effective counter displays, and by making use of skillful point-of-purchase advertising.

2. *Marketing continuity:* Rather than concentrate on short-term promotions, Berkey has worked to create themes, slogans, and brand names that endure. This helps cement relationships with the stores that carry Berkey processing. It also protects Berkey against market entrants.

Figure 11. One Company's Competitive Advantage

tages exist—it will help you to focus on the competitive advantages in your industry. Competitive advantages serve one of two purposes:

They improve a company's position in relation to another market participant.

They discourage companies without the advantage from entering the market.

Use Competitive Analysis Worksheet 14 to evaluate each of these advantages in relation to your competitors. The ones that are most applicable to your business should become focal points for your competitor analysis, especially when examining those competitors who are strongest in each particular area.

1. Differentiation. This refers to real or perceived differences between one company's product and that of its competitors. Differentiation may be a result of a product's uniqueness—Polaroid possessed a significant competitive advantage as long as it had a

. . . .

Information Key

If differentiation is a competitive advantage in your industry, consider the ways in which your own products' differentiation addresses particular market segments. How do your principal competitor's products "fit" in

Your Product Category	Market Segment Addressed	Fit: Good/Fair/ Poor

Your Competitor's Product Category	Market Segment Addressed	Fit: Good/Fair/ Poor

. . . .

patent on instant photography. Or it may be the result of an apparent uniqueness, as is the case with Chanel No. 5 and other expensive perfumes. Brand names are the main tools of differentiation. In one recent year Kellogg's, the breakfast cereal producer, generated a 28 percent return on equity, largely because its brand names differentiate its products from those of competitors. The company maintains this advantage through heavy advertising and promotion.

Besides using brand names, a company can differentiate its products through their features or characteristics. Canon introduced electronic controls to set apart its cameras from other similar 35mm varieties. Scott Paper introduced a paper towel in a new size in order to differentiate it from the standard 11-inch-width products of competitors.

Differentiation often parallels segmentation. A company can obtain an advantage by differentiating a product in such a way that it appeals to a particular market segment. Auto companies have identified market segments of buyers interested in high-performance cars, utilitarian cars, and luxury vehicles. They differentiate one group of products from another in order to appeal to these defined segments.

2. Economy of Scale. This is a clear advantage in many businesses, from papermaking to parcel delivery. The advantage can come through manufacturing efficiencies, as in the chemical and automobile industries. Or it can arise from marketing efficiencies, as in food processing and cigarettes. Economies in purchasing, research, transportation, and many other areas can result from a large-scale operation.

When considering this factor as a competitive advantage, remember that limits exist to economies of scale. While the large computer companies have abundant resources and structures to support research, a disproportionate amount of innovative technology has been developed by smaller firms. To be an advantage, scale economies must be manageable and not offset by accompanying disadvantages.

3. Other Cost Advantages. The Great Lakes Chemical Corp. possesses a competitive advantage in the bromine-based chemicals market by owning a plentiful supply of the raw materials used in their manufacture. Timken Co. gained cost advantages over its competitors by both recycling energy and negotiating labor agreements that allowed more flexible work rules. Proprietary products, process improvements, better inventory management, and many other factors can provide a company with lower costs than its rivals. These advantages can then be translated into market success by means of lower prices or higher quality.

4. Distribution. Gillette, when it entered the cigarette lighter market, had an advantage over other entrants due to the fact that it already had access to efficient channels of distribution that it had developed in its razor business. Having a better or cheaper way of getting your products to customers will often provide you with a significant advantage over your competitors. Auto companies long had a major distribution advantage by possessing exclusive dealerships. Market entrants without this network of outlets faced a tough competitive fight.

5. Product Quality. In some fields, product quality is the primary competitive factor. Hewlett-Packard is known for the high quality of its

. . . .

The competitive advantages of technology are not confined to companies in computer-oriented "Silicon Valley." Procter & Gamble grew out of a candle-making business and still enjoys large revenues from its Ivory soap product which was introduced in 1879. But despite being in a "low-tech" business, the company has always used technology as part of its competitive advantage.

Says Procter & Gamble vice-chairman Thomas Laco: "A lot of analysts criticize companies for being too short-term oriented. What you see at P&G is just the opposite. We will make short-term sacrifices to make sure the technology we bring to market is as effective as possible to give us long-term success."

Besides originating synthetic detergents and disposable diapers (Procter & Gamble still controls approximately 50 percent of the U.S. market for both items), the company recently introduced an orange juice brand based on a new processing technology. It is currently working on developing powdered carbonated soft drinks and a new food product—sucrose polyester—that helps reduce blood cholesterol. Procter & Gamble's example points to the fact that technical developments can pay off in almost any industry.

. . . .

scientific instruments. Steinway and Sons has been successful in the piano market because of the consistent high quality and hand-made nature of its products. U.S. integrated circuit producers like National Semiconductor suffered in the late 1970s because the quality of their products was perceived as lower than comparable Japanese circuits.

6. Technology. Originating technology breakthroughs, or applying existing technology to new areas, can provide important competitive advantages. AT&T, relying on the research capabilities of its Bell Labs division, has maintained a consistent advantage in technology. 3M has relied on its ability to apply technology to diverse areas in order to remain competitive in its wide-ranging businesses.

7. Pricing Strategy. The crucial nature of price in attracting customers while at the same time providing a profitable return to the seller makes this an important competitive area. For example, Texas Instruments was able to achieve great success in producing microcircuits by basing its price on the cost associated with an expected future volume. This strategy of "pricing down the learning curve" enabled the firm to capture market share from competitors.

8. Integration. Besides spreading overhead and providing economies of scale, integration can assure access to both supplies and distribution systems.

9. Geography. A company that is closer to its markets than its competitors, closer to resources or suppliers, or is located in an area of cheap labor, will have a definite competitive advantage. Aluminum producers with plants in the northwestern U.S. have the advantage of abundant, inexpensive hydroelectric power nearby. A company like Sealed Power, which makes original and replacement auto parts, benefits from its location in Michigan near the automotive industry center in Detroit.

10. Switching Costs. Many means of creating competitive advantages through switching costs are available. Companies sell machinery systems to discourage customers from purchasing individual components from competitors. A word processing equipment maker may provide training for a customer's employees. Afterward, retraining the employees to use a competitor's products will require further time and money. All switching costs tend to produce a competitive advantage by increasing customer loyalty and repeat business.

11. Access to Capital. Consider two companies entering the cable television market. One is an independent start-up firm, the other a division of a large, diversified corporation. The business requires substantial investment. Cash flow develops slowly. Which firm has the competitive advantage? Clearly the one that can draw on the capital resources of its parent firm in order to establish and upgrade its cable system.

Access to capital, which may result from good banking relationships, a low debt/equity ratio, or a conservative liquidity position, can be an important factor in many competitive situations. New technology may require substantial investment in order to keep up with rivals. A price war may deplete retained earnings. An economic recession may dry

Action Probes

In what ways can you build in more switching costs to help retain customers who might otherwise switch to competitors?

Can you modify your products in such a way that switching costs are reduced for competitors' customers who might then begin buying from you?

. . . .

up cash flow. In each case, the company with the greatest capital resources has the advantage.

12. Management. The skill, experience, imagination, and depth of a company's management constitutes an important advantage over a company whose executives are not as capable. Sometimes the difference can rest on one individual—Henry Ford II at Ford Motor or Ray Kroc at McDonald's—sometimes on a whole system of management—such as those that exist at General Electric and 3M.

13. Organization. Is one competitor better organized to serve particular markets? Does one company's structure facilitate flexibility in the face of change? Is a company built around manufacturing when marketing skills are most important? A decentralized organization may give a company a competitive boost because it allows the firm to respond more quickly to customer needs. Centralization, on the other hand, may prove an advantage by allowing for better cost control. Organization can become a competitive advantage to the extent that it is suited to the industry conditions the company faces.

14. Government Intervention. During a recent year, the U.S. steel industry spent $651 million on antipollution measures, 19.3 percent of its total capital investment. The Japanese steel industry spent $321 million, 11.5 percent of its investment. This government-mandated differential contributed to the competitive advantage of the Japanese firms. Other government policies, from direct financial aid to tariff protection for home markets, can create or increase competitive strength.

15. Service. A supermarket takes business from its competitors

Information Key

Put yourself in the place of a customer just entering your market. He is trying to decide whether to purchase from your company or from your principal competitor. What competitive advantages does each firm possess in the struggle to attract his business?

Your company's advantages: _____

_____

Your competitor's advantages: _____

_____

because it offers free delivery. A manufacturer is able to sell a conveyor belt system because it promises customers that it will provide engineers to help install the product and get it running properly. Service can provide a key advantage in industries ranging from hotels to computers, from airlines to oil-well servicing.

Charting Your Competitors

Competitive advantages are sometimes clear and obvious, other times hard to distinguish. Multiple factors are usually involved in bringing success to one firm and failure to another. In order to help you to determine who the winners and losers among your competitors are, chart various characteristics of companies against each other.

For example, you might want to know the relationship of revenue size to profitability. Set up a chart that plots sales against return on sales. Chart A in Figure 12 shows a situation in which larger firms are generally more profitable. This might indicate the advantage of economies of scale. Chart B shows a situation in which both very small and very large firms show higher profitability. Here, smaller firms may be serving more profitable specialty niches, while the largest companies rely on manufacturing efficiencies. Companies caught in between lack either competitive advantage.

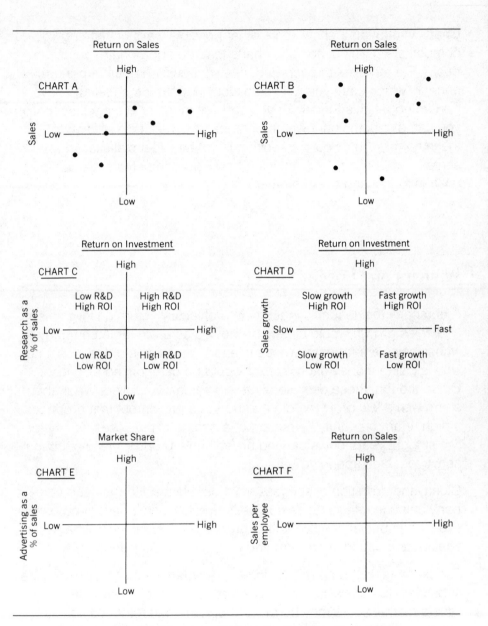

Figure 12. Six Charts to Reflect Competitive Capabilities

Charts C through F show some other possible ways of charting your competitors. Think of specific charts that are appropriate for your industry. For the axes of each grid, use your own company's performance, in which case you will see exactly how your competitors have performed relative to you. Or you can use industry averages so that you can plot both your own and competitor's results in relation to these norms. What you are seeking is not an exact statistical representation, but a tool for examining how your competitors are doing in relation to you and to each other.

Winners and Losers

A company that leads its industry in profitability, return on investment, and sales growth would clearly be viewed as a winner. A company whose sales are lagging, whose financial situation is precarious, and who is losing money each quarter would be categorized as a loser. Often, though, these definitions are not so easily applied. What about a firm with a low profit margin and no sales growth but that produces a high return on equity? What about a company that loses money for two straight years but is carving out valuable product niches through heavy research spending?

Clearly the definition of success must be relative. How is each company doing in relation to its competitors? How has it performed relative to the special conditions that prevail in every market? What weight should be given to short-term and long-term performance?

For example, in the petroleum industry, immediate profitability may be subsidiary to acquisition of oil reserves. In consumer products, establishing market share may be more important than return on assets. The hiring of key sales personnel may be a critical measure of success in a service business like stock brokerage. Successful research and development may be the overwhelming definer of success in semiconductors or pharmaceuticals. A book publishing company recently went bankrupt because management spent too much time on

Information Key

Often it's easy to name the winners in your industry, but harder to specify the exact criteria that determine why they shoud be so labeled. Write down the names of the three most successful competitors in your industry, then add the reason you selected each one:

Company	Reason
1. _____	_____
2. _____	_____
3. _____	_____

one success factor—gaining access to capital—and not enough on an even more critical measure—acquisition of books to publish.

When you rate the success of your own competitors, you have to take the multiple facets of your industry into consideration. Competitive Analysis Worksheet 15 helps you list the winners and losers in your competitive environment. Incorporate your thoughts from the Information Key above. Be sure to consider whether the competitor is a long or short-term winner or loser.

The following list will help your thinking about this question:

Winners	Competitive Advantages
Sony	Product innovation, quality
McDonald's	Quality, standardization, economies of scale
Anheuser-Busch	Economies of scale, marketing skill
Rite-Aid (drugstores)	Store size, marketing emphasis on high-margin prescription drugs
Iowa Beef Processors	Innovative packaging, low costs

Losers	Competitive Disadvantages
Addressograph-Multigraph	Failure to respond to technical innovation
Warwick (color television)	Manufacturing and management inefficiency (Sanyo took over the Warwick plants and operated them profitably)
Draper (textile machinery)	Lack of research investment
W.T. Grant (discount stores)	Lack of marketing focus, poor merchandising strategy

COMPETITIVE ANALYSIS WORKSHEET 12

MARKET PROFILE

Market definition: _____

Our sales last year: _____   Percent of our total sales: _____%

Our operating profits: _____   Percent of total: _____%

A. Concentration

	Volume of Market Share	Percent of Total Market
Total market	_____	100%
Our company	_____	_____
Competitor _____	_____	_____
Competitor _____	_____	_____
Competitor _____	_____	_____
Competitor _____	_____	_____
Top 5 participants	_____	_____
Top 10 participants	_____	_____
Top 50 participants	_____	_____
Total number of participants: _____		

B. Segmentation

Segment 1: _____

   Special characteristics: _____

   Segment leader: _____

Segment 2: _____

   Special characteristics: _____

   Segment leader: _____

Segment 3: _____

   Special characteristics: _____

   Segment leader: _____

C. Market Growth

	Reported Growth	Real Growth (corrected for inflation)
Our revenues (this market) past year	_____	_____
Total market past year	_____	_____
Average yearly growth past five years	_____	_____
Estimated growth next year	_____	_____
Estimated average growth next five years	_____	_____

Price trend in market: ____ Higher ____ Stable ____ Lower

D. Geographic Parameters

This market is best classified as:

____ Local ____ Regional ____ Domestic ____ International

Geographic boundaries of market: _____

_____

Geographic constraints on market expansion: _____

_____

Possible ways of overcoming constraints: _____

_____

_____

_____

COMPETITIVE ANALYSIS WORKSHEET 13

COMPETITOR CHECKLIST

List the competitive threat posed by companies according to the following scale:

    1—Urgent threat; requires immediate attention
    2—Serious threat; requires close observation and analysis
    3—Possible threat; track closely for developments
    4—Unlikely threat at this time.

A. Current Market Participants

Company	Competitive Threat	Market Share Percent	Share is: Growing/ Declining	Company is: Specialist/ Generalist
_____	_____	_____	_____	_____
_____	_____	_____	_____	_____
_____	_____	_____	_____	_____
_____	_____	_____	_____	_____
_____	_____	_____	_____	_____

B. Potential Entrants

1. Companies entering through geographic expansion:

Company	Competitive Threat	Currently Operates in (Locations)	Company is: Specialist/ Generalist
_____	_____	_____	_____
_____	_____	_____	_____
_____	_____	_____	_____
_____	_____	_____	_____

2. Suppliers who could integrate forward:

Company	Competitive Threat	Currently Supplies Materials, Components	Likelihood of Integration (High, Medium, Low)
_____	_____	_____	_____
_____	_____	_____	_____
_____	_____	_____	_____
_____	_____	_____	_____

3. Customers who could integrate backward:

Company	Competitive Threat	Currently Purchases (Products)	Likelihood of Market Entry (High, Medium, Low)
_____	_____	_____	_____
_____	_____	_____	_____
_____	_____	_____	_____
_____	_____	_____	_____

4. Related companies which could enter via horizontal integration:

Company	Competitive Threat	Relationship to Market	Likelihood of Market Entry (High, Medium, Low)
_____	_____	_____	_____
_____	_____	_____	_____
_____	_____	_____	_____
_____	_____	_____	_____

C. Substitute Products

Substitute Product	Major Producer	Competitive Threat

COMPETITIVE ANALYSIS WORKSHEET 14

COMPETITIVE ADVANTAGE CHECKLIST

Advantage	Applies to Our Market: Yes/No	Operates via: Improved Position	Operates via: Discourages Entry	Competitor with Best Position	Our Position (Good, Fair, Poor)
1. Differentiation					
2. Economy of scale					
3. Other cost					
4. Distribution					
5. Product quality					
6. Technology					
7. Pricing					
8. Integration					
9. Geography					
10. Switching costs					
11. Access to capital					
12. Management					
13. Organization					
14. Government intervention					
15. Service					

Other:

_____

_____

_____

_____

COMPETITIVE ANALYSIS WORKSHEET 15

MARKET WINNERS AND LOSERS

Winners

Company 1: _____   Specialist: ___   Generalist: ___

   Market share: _____ percent

   Principal indicators of success: **1.** _____

                                     2. _____

                                     3. _____

   Main competitive advantages: _____

   Time frame: Long-term ___   Short-term ___   Both ___

Company 2: _____   Specialist: ___   Generalist: ___

   Market share: _____ percent

   Principal indicators of success: **1.** _____

                                     2. _____

                                     3. _____

   Main competitive advantages: _____

   Time frame: Long-term ___   Short-term ___   Both ___

Losers

Company 1: _____   Specialist ___   Generalist: ___

   Market Share: ___ percent

   Principal indicators of failure: **1.** _____

                                     2. _____

                                     3. _____

   Main competitive disadvantages: _____

   Time frame: Long-term ___   Short-term ___   Both ___

11

How to Evaluate a Competitor's Operations

C hapters 11, 12, and 13 guide you through detailed evaluations of each of your principal competitors. Once you have completed the Competitive Analysis Worksheets in these chapters you will have a clear view not only of the competition's operations, administration, finances, and strategy, but also of their various strengths and weaknesses in each area. This information will lead you directly to competitive moves to exploit their vulnerable points and prepare effective defenses to neutralize their strengths.

You should fill out a full set of Competitive Analysis Worksheets for each major competitor or for each distinct business unit of a diversified company. If a competitor has several separate and distinct product lines, you might find it easier to reproduce the Worksheets in Chapter 11 and fill in one for each line.

Adapt the wording of the forms to the type of industry in which you compete. For example, if you are in the retail business, substitute "store" for "plant" and "square feet of area" for "capacity." As always, substitute "service" for "product" if you are in a service industry.

When you've completed the forms, gather them together into a *Competitor Profile.* Eventually you will compile more information than is called for in these sheets, especially in connection with key competitive factors. But your Competitor Profile will give you a convenient summary of the most important competitive data. Update it frequently and make sure it is available to decision makers in your company.

Tips on Analysis

1. Always keep competitive advantages in mind. What is important? A competitor may be poor in his advertising effort, but if advertising is a negligible factor in your industry, this weakness has little significance.

2. Strengths and Weaknesses are the heart of each Competitive Analysis Worksheet. Recognize that the terms are relative. A strength is a factor that allows a competitor to attract or hold customers better than you can, or to compete more proficiently in some other way. A weakness is a factor that gives you an advantage over him.

Be particularly careful to look for *potential* strengths and weaknesses. A competitor may have allowed his sales force to grow lax. While he isn't losing any market share yet, an increased effort by your sales reps may be able to exploit this weakness. On the other hand, a large bank line of credit represents a potential strength. You'll have to watch how the competitor uses the capital and be ready to counter his moves.

3. As a starter exercise, fill in the Competitive Analysis Worksheets for your own company. This gives you a base of comparison. It also provides a chance to take an objective look at your firm from the point of view of a competitor.

4. Use estimates when you don't have actual facts. Mark each estimated figure (e.g., sales: $125,000 (e)). Better to use educated guesses than to leave spaces blank. As you gather more data, refine your figures. But don't waste time trying to pin down exact numbers.

5. Look for trends. A market share leader whose sales are flat may not represent as important a competitive threat as a company with a smaller share whose sales are growing rapidly. Competitor analysis is dynamic, not static.

Competitor's History

Vital Statistics

Competitive Analysis Worksheet 16 deals with the background of the competitor company. Begin by filling in the firm's vital statistics in Part A. These facts serve as a reference, but also have competitive implications. Ownership is important.

For example, a large block of the stock of the A&P supermarket chain was owned for years by a foundation set up by the company's founder. Many analysts viewed this arrangement as detrimental to the independence of the company's management and as a significant

· ·

Information Key

Take a map that includes the competitor's area of operation and locate all his plants, offices, warehouses, and other facilities. Plot the location of major suppliers, customers, and transportation routes as well. This will be a valuable visual aid in analyzing his operations.

· ·

factor in the firm's decline. Whether the competitor is a public or private company, whether the owner is an entrepreneur or a financially conservative family—these facts will influence how the company competes.

Geography

Part B of Competitive Analysis Worksheet 16 details the geographic alignment of the company. Some of the competitive implications of geography were discussed in Chapter 10. A good example of the competitive influence of geography occurred when deregulation hit the airline industry. Eastern Air Lines operated its most profitable routes in the dense East Coast corridor. Since these routes were hit hardest by new low-cost competitors, such as People Express and New York Air, Eastern suffered substantial loss of market share and revenue.

Major Events

Next consider the major events (Part C) that have played a role in the company's development, particularly during recent years. Has the company made a significant acquisition that it's still trying to digest? Has it undergone a disaster that is likely to hamper its ability to compete for some time to come?

In 1984 Union Carbide suffered a major disaster at its pesticide plant in India. Think about how this affected the company's plant location tactics, management controls, spending on safety features, financial health, and so forth.

Successes and Failures

Some companies repeat failures, some learn from them. Some shun opportunities in areas where they've previously failed. For example, Federated Department Stores long delayed its entry into discounting after failing in the area. Texas Instruments, on the other hand, twice tried and failed to succeed in consumer products.

Success can also influence competitive behavior. Some companies stick to what they do well and continue their success. Others over-extend themselves in the direction of previous successes, ignoring clear danger signals.

What important successes and failures has your competitor experienced? Can you identify a pattern? What have the consequences been? Record this information in Part D of Competitive Analysis Worksheet 16.

Reputation

This category tends to sum up a great many intangible factors about the firm. You always have to question whether a company will live up to its reputation in the future. But evaluating reputation can be helpful in analysis.

Use Part E of Competitive Analysis Worksheet 16 to record your views on the competitor's reputation. Update this analysis as you gain wider data on how the company is regarded.

Strengths and Weaknesses

The last section of this Competitive Analysis Worksheet asks you to identify the competitor's strengths and weaknesses that emerge from a look at its history. Be as specific as possible. Don't say "overcautious management." Instead, write: "Failure of product X has made the company's managers shy away from products involving new technology."

. . . .

Action Probes

Can you use the fact that you've been in business longer than the competitor as a selling tool?

Have you been ready to take advantage of disruptions to a competitor's operations (e.g., as a result of a strike) in order to gain market share?

. . . .

Competitor's Products

Product Lines

Competitive Analysis Worksheet 17 will help you to evaluate the competitor's products. Begin by filling in Part A, which provides a summary of each of its product lines. The important thing to note here is the contribution that each line makes to the company's sales and profits. This will give you an idea of the commitment the firm has to the line.

Look as well at the customer groups that are most important in each product area. Compare them to your own customer alignment. How important are principal customers to the competitor? If the company sells largely to a few customers, it is likely to put up a fierce competitive battle for their business.

Product Leadership

Part B of Worksheet 17 asks you to identify the areas in which the competitor is a market leader—that is, has the largest portion of market sales. Market leadership has important competitive implications. IBM, for example, is able to disrupt competitors' marketing plans simply by announcing that it is developing a new product. Customers will delay their purchase decisions until they can examine the market leader's offering.

Include a brief explanation of how the competitor attained leadership: through technology breakthroughs, marketing skill, low-cost produc-

· ·

Information Key

Get an idea of the importance of leadership in your industry by comparing the return on investment of three high market share companies and three lower market share firms. Try to choose typical companies.

High Market Share Companies	Share	ROI	Low Market Share Companies	Share	ROI
1. _____	_____	_____	1. _____	_____	_____
2. _____	_____	_____	2. _____	_____	_____
3. _____	_____	_____	3. _____	_____	_____

· ·

tion? Ask yourself not only who the leaders in your market are, but what leadership means.

Dimensions of Product Line

Part C of Competitive Analysis Worksheet 17 evaluates whether the competitor is a full-line producer or is niche-oriented. The major U.S. auto companies are an example of full-line firms—they offer products in each market segment. Department stores are full-line retailers. Generally, full-line competitors attempt to achieve large volume and to standardize their product offerings.

Niche-oriented companies offer a limited line of products but may have greater depth—more varieties of a particular type of product. Volkswagen is an example of a company that succeeded with a niche orientation, specializing in smaller, low-end cars.

Width and depth of product line will influence how the company competes. Niche orientation may be useful for gaining entry to a market and building a base. Honda started out as a niche player in motorcycles, gradually expanding into a full line. In disposable diapers, Procter & Gamble recently reduced the breadth of their line, specializing in premium products as it saw customers gravitating toward either the high end or to low-priced generics.

Product Strategy

Consider some of the possible strategies that your competitor may adopt and their effects:

Companies with *unique* products—Polaroid's instant photography, pharmaceutical firms' proprietary drugs—may be vulnerable to competition because of their lack of attention to marketing, or because they try to overextend a single technology. Or they may lack the capital to maintain the level of research needed to supply them with a stream of unique products.

Firms that rely on *differentiation* can be attacked through products that duplicate the features of their successful models. Kodak's disc camera very quickly spawned many imitators.

A *standardization* strategy—Gillette in razor blades, Kodak in film, IBM in computers—requires competitors to adapt their own product strategy accordingly. Schick, Fuji, and plug-compatible data processing companies have done so successfully.

In Part D of Competitive Analysis Worksheet 17 check the strategy that best characterizes this competitor's approach. Then look at a number of that company's products and examine how it is carrying out the strategy in practice.

Now stop for a minute and sum up the strengths and weaknesses you see in the competitor's product line and strategy. Remember that strengths and weaknesses may be closely related. A full-line approach creates a broad customer franchise—but it also leaves the company vulnerable at many points to attacks by niche-oriented companies. Market leadership can result in manufacturing efficiencies—but it can also leave the competitor less flexible in the face of new technology or demand changes.

Action Probes

In which product areas is the competitor most vulnerable?

How can you focus attacks on these particular points that will improve your position across the board?

. . . .

Product Quality

Evaluate each of the competitor's main product lines for quality in Part E of Competitive Analysis Worksheet 17. Are there immediate problems you could exploit? Is the competitor building in more quality than necessary?

Consider quality from a customer's point of view. An appliance maker noted that while workmanship on a competitor's ranges was adequate, the quality of the design was deficient. Users had to reach over hot burners to operate the controls. By locating its own controls more conveniently, the company obtained a competitive advantage.

Service

Part F of Competitive Analysis Worksheet 17 contains questions about the competitor's service. Some competitors may use service as a marketing tool. Others may see it as a source of revenue. For example, an office equipment dealer may offer service contracts on its equipment that over time yield greater profits than the equipment sales themselves.

Sometimes service is priced separately, other times it is bundled into the price of the purchase, as when warranties are included. How does this affect competition?

Computer dealers offer presale service in the form of seminars on how to select the right machine. This may give them a sales edge over rivals.

Once you've completed this section, examine where the competitor's

. . . .

Action Probes

In what area is your product most superior in quality to the competitor's? How can you exploit this superiority?

Is a large block of customers looking for a *lower* quality product at a lower price? Could you develop a product for this market?

If a competitor sells service, could you bundle it into the price of the product and then offer it for "free"?

. . . .

strengths and weaknesses are in terms of quality and service. Is its quality virtually unassailable so that a competitor had best yield a product area and find a more attractive niche? Is its service slow even though customers rate fast service highly?

Product Development

Part G of Competitive Analysis Worksheet 17 focuses your attention on the competitor's strategy for developing new products. Some companies, like Procter & Gamble, are leaders in product development and bring out a succession of new products and improvements. Others make no effort to introduce entirely new products but rely on coming out with versions of products pioneered by others. Sony has traditionally followed this pattern. Still other firms succeed by applying established technology to new fields. The many applications of microcircuits illustrate this tack.

At what rate does the competitor bring out new products? Campbell Soup is aggressive in this area, launching 334 products in the past five years. How does your competitor approach the question of product development? Are new product ideas treated carefully? Or does the company look only for those ideas promising a quick payoff?

Research Efforts

Look at the specifics of the competitor's research (Part H of Competitive Analysis Worksheet 17). The structure of its research organization

Information Key

List four recent new products that the competitor has introduced and note the success of each:

Product	Result
1. _____	_____
2. _____	_____
3. _____	_____
4. _____	_____

will have competitive implications. A company with its own R&D department has full control and can direct the research toward specific ends. But it will have to devote a certain amount of capital to this purpose in order to be effective. Other means, such as joint ventures or licensing, may slow product introductions and reduce flexibility, but could also be more cost-effective.

Here are some examples of competitive effects related to research:

Merck & Co. recently purchased two Japanese companies that specialize in antibiotic and dermatological drugs.

Competitive effect: By drawing on the research of these new subsidiaries, Merck will increase its ability to compete in these areas.

BSR, once the world's largest maker of phonographs, virtually neglected research into new technology.

Competitive effect: Competitors were able to introduce features which eventually drove BSR out of the business.

What are your competitor's strengths and weaknesses in product development and research? Does it invest too heavily to develop new products that have minimal proprietary value and are subject to intense competition early? Does it make effective use of development funds by applying already proven technology to new areas? Consider this important area carefully. Record your conclusions on Competitive Analysis Worksheet 17.

Marketing

Competitive Analysis Worksheet 18 deals with the competitor's marketing. Use Part A to sketch a general view of how well the competitor markets its products to customers. For example, does it thoroughly research customer needs? Companies like Eastman Kodak, which tested 63 different designs on 2,227 subjects before introducing its disc camera, tend to be in close touch with their customers.

How does the competitor make use of its brand names? Coca-Cola has been extremely careful not to dilute the value of its Coke trademark. When it finally did use it for another product, Diet Coke became an enormous success.

List the company's marketing strengths and weaknesses immediately. Then, as you examine other factors, look for areas of potential competitive advantage that result from them.

Promotion

Detail your competitor's promotional strategies in Part B of Competitive Analysis Worksheet 18. Begin by looking at the company's image as put across in promotion and advertising. Is it clear and consistent? More companies are following the lead of General Motors, which backs up its separate brands with a strong company image, and Panasonic, which markets a wide variety of products under a common name, image, and slogan. Beatrice has just begun to use this tactic with its food products.

Look at the competitive implications of the mix of promotion tactics. For example, studies show that neither advertising nor in-store promotion is sufficient to sell soft drinks effectively. A mixture of the two is best. Is your competitor spending its promotional budget in the most efficient way?

What advertising agency does the firm use? What are *its* strengths and weaknesses? How does it fit with the company's promotional strategy?

Every day your competitor is making marketing decisions: Should it concentrate on push or pull advertising? Are educational or highly factual promotional activities needed, or should the theme be emotional? Should advertising be constant or focused on selling opportunities? Evaluate each element and see where the firm is failing or succeeding.

Promotion as a Competitive Weapon

Wendy's, the fast food chain, presents a good example of the competitive implications of promotion. The company recently drastically reduced discount coupons—a standby in the industry—and focused on television advertising. Distinctive advertisements, such as one challenging competitors with the slogan "Where's the beef?" helped boost Wendy's 1984 sales by 27 percent.

The increased awareness that can be created through television fit with Wendy's marketing strategy. Because it has fewer restaurants than rivals McDonald's and Burger King, it needs to create awareness in order to induce customers to travel farther to its facilities.

This case shows that it is the astute use of promotional activities, not the volume of spending, that is important. Both of Wendy's competitors spent far more on promotion, but neither gained the same results.

Sum up the competitor's strengths and weaknesses in promotion. Look beyond the surface to consider in-store displays, effectiveness at trade shows, media selection, and so forth.

Distribution

Next look at distribution channels and fill in Part C of Competitive Analysis Worksheet 18. Which distribution channels does the competi-

. . . .

Action Probes

Can you use advertising media that the competitor is neglecting (e.g., billboards) in order to increase the relative awareness of your products?

Would more detailed market research show you how to reach particular customer groups more effectively than competitors?

. . . .

tor use? Which does it neglect? Why? How many intermediaries handle the firm's products?

Tandy has been successful in eliminating middlemen and selling its consumer electronics products directly through its Radio Shack outlets. Lafayette, another electronics manufacturer who tried the same thing, went bankrupt. Eliminating middlemen can cut selling price, but it limits the company's available outlets.

Keep a close eye on the competitive implications of distribution patterns. For example:

> Caterpillar Tractor has chosen to cut prices in order to protect its valuable network of dealers. Competitors have to be aware of Caterpillar's determination to preserve this distribution system.

> The Steiger Tractor Company had been distributing its 4-wheel drive tractors through International Harvester dealers. When the International Harvester agricultural business was sold to Tenneco, that company merged it into its I.J. Case subsidiary which already sold its own 4-wheel drive products. Steiger was left without a distribution network and suffered severe competitive consequences.

> General Foods recently began selling gourmet food products through direct mail. Analysts see this distribution outlet growing in importance. General Foods competitors have already begun studying how they can also participate.

Distribution Switch Leads to Competitive Success
California Coolers, Inc. became the fourth largest wine shipper in the state, quickly achieving $72 million in revenues, by selecting a novel distribution method. Rather than use the traditional wine outlets, the

company packaged its product in 12-ounce bottles and distributed it through beer and soft drink dealers who service convenience stores. This tactic allowed the company to reach its target market very effectively. Getting the jump on competitors, it captured two-thirds of the wine-cooler market.

Sales

Analog Devices, a manufacturer of electronic components, obtained a great competitive advantage over its rivals by hiring experienced engineers as salespeople. These reps were able to sell more effectively with their in-depth understanding of customer needs. They also provided important new product suggestions because they could spot areas in which new needs would develop.

Fill in the details about your competitor's sales force in Part D of Competitive Analysis Worksheet 18. Pay attention to how the sales reps are organized. Does each offer the company's full line in a particular geographic territory? Are they responsible for selling particular types of products? Does this create inefficiencies through duplication of efforts? Are they organized by customer groups? Are some groups being ignored?

How are salespeople compensated? A straight commission arrangement, for example, may encourage them to ignore low-volume customers. Sales compensation can be used as a competitive tactic. AT&T's sales staff sells both telephone products and its new microcomputer. In order to stimulate computer sales, the company bases half of the sales rep's commission on his sale of computers and half on his efforts with other products.

Pricing

Pricing strategy and tactics are a vital area of interest for executives conducting competitor analysis because they so often represent the "front line" of the competitive battle. Competitive Analysis Worksheet

. . . .

Information Key

Imagine one of your salespeople and one from a principal rival approaching an important potential customer on the same day. How would their sales techniques and emphases differ? What advantage would each have to win the account?

Your Salesperson   Competitor's Salesperson
_____   _____

Approach: _____   Approach: _____

_____   _____

Advantages: _____   Advantages: _____

_____   _____

. . . .

19 will help you organize the information you gather about a competitor's pricing activity.

Position

Part A of Competitive Analysis Worksheet 19 looks at the competitor's price position. Is it generally high? Low? Or does the firm follow the industry average? Low-price participants tend to seek higher volume. They may also be attempting to establish a base in terms of market share. People Express, a cut-rate airline, was a good example of both facets—its low prices allowed it to fill planes and to rapidly expand routes and facilities. Higher-price competitors suffered.

Low-price competitors may also be engaged in "cream skimming." Here, the company specializes in a profitable market niche. High margins allow it to cut prices, attract customers from full-line competitors, and still operate profitably. MCI used this strategy when it offered limited long-distance phone service at lower rates than AT&T.

A high-price position usually results from proprietary technology (as with prescription pharmaceutical producers), high quality (Mercedes Benz), strong differentiation (perfume, premium beer), or other factors such as reputation, dependability, or service. Competitively, a high-price position runs the risk of attracting lower-price competitors. For example, Caterpillar Tractor has encountered competition from Komatsu, Ltd.—a company producing similar quality heavy equipment but selling below Caterpillar's price.

Strategy

Look even more closely at the competitor's price strategy and fill in Part B of Competitive Analysis Worksheet 19. Has the company established clear price points for its products, or is the pattern confused? IBM lowered the price of its XT personal computer partly to prevent a "price collision" with the more powerful AT model. Which of the following seem to be the goals of the competitor's price strategy?

1. Total Cost Pricing. In this case, the company aims for a particular profit margin, which it then tacks onto the cost of production and overhead in order to arrive at a selling price.

2. Capacity Pricing. This structure is based on the need to keep its factories running at capacity. Makers of commodity products, such as corrugated packaging, may sell to high-volume customers at prices below total cost in order to keep production up. Profits come from higher prices charged to smaller customers.

3. Value Pricing. This strategy focuses on customers. Selling prices vary according to the value of the product to the buyer. This accounts for the higher prices commanded by strongly differentiated products.

4. Learning Curve Pricing. Used particularly with new products, this strategy bases price not on current costs but on future costs which are assumed to be lower as a result of volume and production experience. It sacrifices immediate return for future market share.

Tactics

Part C of Competitive Analysis Worksheet 19 looks at specific pricing tactics. What posture does the company take regarding day-to-day

. . . .

Information Key

Compare your most important product with a comparable product of your principal competitor:

	Your Product	Competitor's Product
Product	_____	_____
Price	_____	_____
Price position	_____	_____
Price strategy	_____	_____

. . . .

price fluctuations? Is the firm a price leader, introducing changes that then spread through the market? Does it follow quickly the moves of the leader? Is it slow to go along with price fluctuations? Do its pricing moves tend to be defensive reactions to competitors' moves? Or does it aggressively cut prices to gain market share? Does the company try to come in at a lower price, or to offer more for the same price?

How consistent are the competitor's price tactics? Does it change prices frequently in response to market factors? Does the company maintain its position, as a low-price producer for example, or do its prices tend to vacillate relative to industry averages?

Control of pricing decisions can have competitive implications. If sales managers or individual salespeople enjoy considerable latitude in pricing, the company may be quick to respond to fluctuations, but it may also be vulnerable in terms of margin erosion and price confusion. Top management control will usually yield a more rational strategy, but is less flexible.

What does the price include? The Japanese used bundling tactics in invading the U.S. auto market, offering what had been expensive options on American cars as standard features at a price that was lower than comparable U.S. auto company prices.

Pricing tactics may not be solely confined to selling price. An equipment manufacturer, by offering buyers low-interest loans to finance their purchases, is actually introducing a price differential. Rebates, credit terms, warranties, and other features can serve as hidden price cuts.

Direct discounts are also an aspect of price tactics. When does the competitor tend to resort to off-pricing? To attract key customers? In the case of quantity orders? When sales slow? To reduce overstocks?

Now evaluate the strengths and weaknesses of the competitor's overall price moves. What competitive openings does it leave? How has its pricing strategy helped its overall market approach?

Pricing Parry in Potato Chips

Frito-Lay encountered a clever use of pricing as a competitive weapon after it offered a larger quantity of potato chips at a higher price point (but at a lower per-ounce price). A number of competitors countered by increasing the size of their bags, keeping the weight of the contents the same, and charging a price lower than Frito's. This made the Frito-Lay price cut appear to the casual shopper to be a price increase, totally frustrating its competitive effect.

Production

Because production conditions vary between facilities, it may well be useful to fill out a copy of Competitive Analysis Worksheet 20 for each of the competitor's plants.

Vital Statistics

Begin by looking at the general features of the plant: its equipment, age, and the advantages and disadvantages apparent in its location and layout. Limited means of transportation, lack of storage space, expensive local utilities, all could have competitive implications. Fill in this information in Part A.

Capacity

Part B of Worksheet 20 concerns the competitor's production capacity. Is the firm aggressive in keeping the plant operating near capacity? U.S. Gypsum recently operated its 25 building supply plants at 97 percent capacity. But it wasn't tempted to rush out and build more capacity. Said company president Robert J. Day: "There's a lot of don'ts. One is, don't build capacity for the peaks. Plan for the next drop."

Does the company have considerable unused capacity available? Will the company be forced to spend heavily in order to increase production? Does it tend to add capacity during periods of high demand and experience overcapacity when sales lag? How does it add capacity?

Boise Cascade gained an advantage on competitors when demand for white paper increased significantly. While other firms constructed new plants, Boise bought and restored older facilities. This enabled the company to increase capacity more quickly and at a lower cost. Dorsey Corp. increased its capacity to produce plastic bottles by placing one extra bottle-making machine in each of its existing plants. This allowed the company to hold down overhead compared to its competitors who built new plants. The tactic had the added advantage of placing the capacity nearer to the markets.

Supply

Part C of Competitive Analysis Worksheet 20 examines the competitor's supply situation. General Motors and Chrysler provide examples of two contrasting approaches to supply. General Motors is an integrated producer making a large proportion of its components in-house. Chrysler has tended to purchase a greater share of its components from outside suppliers.

Action Probes

Can you improve your supply and cost positions by making a component that your competitor purchases?

Have you investigated the possibility of joint ventures with suppliers in order to improve your position in relation to competitors?

Look at your competitor's supply strengths and weaknesses. A manufacturer of electronic components who has trouble obtaining a steady supply of integrated circuits may be vulnerable. A competitor who frequently changes suppliers looking for lower prices may not have a source of materials when demand increases.

Costs

Part D of Competitive Analysis Worksheet 20 will help you evaluate the competitor's costs. Naturally you won't be able to determine its costs as well as you know your own. But by studying diverse sources of information—wage levels in the cities where it has its plants, transportation costs, utility rates, the age of its equipment—you can make good estimates. Astute competitors are aware, for example, that Beatrice is developing a low-cost distribution system as a result of its acquisition of Hunt-Wesson. Eastern Air Lines' competitors know that the company's 1984 wage freeze and productivity drive netted a $50 million cost saving.

Labor productivity is an important cost-related factor in most industries. How does this competitor's productivity compare with yours? With the industry average? How is the company seeking productivity improvements? What will be the competitive implications of this effort?

Now look at the competitor's competitive strengths and weaknesses arising from its cost situation. Does it possess the ability to make competitive gains by lowering prices without losing money? Are its outdated plants forcing its costs up?

Information Key

Use the following chart to focus on the competitor's costs. Base your estimates on annual costs for the most recent year. If you have no information on the costs, make educated guesses.

Fixed Costs		Semi-Variable Costs	
Plant overhead	_____	Research	_____
Administrative	_____	Marketing	_____
Insurance	_____	Maintenance (equipment, etc.)	_____
Property taxes	_____		
General maintenance	_____	Sales	_____
Other: _____	_____	Supervisory salaries	_____
	_____	Other: _____	_____
	_____		_____
Total fixed	_____	Total semi-variable	_____
		Production in units	_____

Variable Costs		Cost per Unit	
Materials	_____	_____	
Labor	_____	_____	
Packaging	_____	_____	
Shipping	_____	_____	
Royalties	_____	_____	
Utilities	_____	_____	
Operating supplies	_____	_____	
Other: _____	_____	_____	
	_____	_____	
Total variable	_____	_____	Total per unit

Additional Production Factors

Inventory management, work flow, and general production skills are another area to consider. The questions in Part E of Competitive Analysis Worksheet 20 can be important ones competitively. For example, a competitor who tries to cut inventory to the bone may leave itself vulnerable to loss of customers because of stockouts.

··

Action Probes

What techniques that you've uncovered by analyzing the competitor's production can you successfully apply to your own operation?

What does an examination of the competitor's production situation tell you about its future options (e.g., it can't quickly increase production, its costs are likely to decline, etc.)? How can you use this knowledge to gain on it competitively?

··

In the past few years, inventory has become the focus of many companies wanting to improve their competitive positions. Consider the following examples:

By applying Japanese "just-in-time" inventory principles, General Motors built a plant in Philadelphia that required only a fraction of the floor space compared to older plants of similar capacity.

Goodyear cut its work-in-progress inventories by a full 50 percent by applying a rigorous modern inventory system.

Texas Instruments has begun giving suppliers annual quantity estimates and committing itself to a two-month supply of goods in order to assure supplies while keeping inventories and delivery problems low.

Look for other production areas in which the competitor has an advantage. For example, does the firm possess particular skills in tooling? Does it use a system of changeover that increases efficiency? Is factory workflow set up in a cost-saving way? Does the firm use materials requirements planning or other computerized systems to boost manufacturing efficiency? Is it particularly adept at avoiding quality problems and rework?

Once you have summed up these advantages, go on to make an overall evaluation of production strengths and weaknesses. Again, remember that the factors may be closely related. A great deal of automation can give the competitor a strength in cost position. But the capital spent on the automation equipment may leave it weaker financially and less flexible in the face of market changes.

COMPETITIVE ANALYSIS WORKSHEET 16

ANALYSIS SHEET: COMPETITOR HISTORY

A. Vital Statistics

Company name: _____

Year founded: _____   Where incorporated: _____

Ownership: _____

Original business: _____

Give a brief account of major developments in the company:

_____

_____

B. Geography

Headquarters address: _____

Geographic focus: ____ Local   ____ National/domestic
                      ____ Regional   ____ International

List all plants, offices, distribution centers, and other facilities:

Facility	Location	Market Area	Year Opened
_____	_____	_____	_____
_____	_____	_____	_____
_____	_____	_____	_____
_____	_____	_____	_____
_____	_____	_____	_____
_____	_____	_____	_____

C. Major Events

Check all the events that have had a significant impact on the company. Explain in the space below or on a separate sheet:

___ Disaster (fire, accident, etc.)	___ Management realignment
___ Strike	___ Bankruptcy
___ Reorganization	___ Financial problems
___ Lawsuit/criminal charges	___ Major new product
___ Relocation	___ Divestiture
___ Entered new market	___ Death, retirement of principal
___ Acquisition/merger	___ Government regulatory action
___ Other: _____	

Details: _____

_____

D. Successes/Failures

What have been the principal successes of the company (products, markets entered, marketing techniques, concepts, ways of doing business, etc.)? Give year, brief description, consequences:

_____

_____

_____

_____

In what areas has the firm experienced significant failures?

_____

_____

_____

_____

How have successes and failures contributed to a pattern of strategic or tactical decisions (e.g., made the firm more defensive)?

_____

_____

_____

_____

E. Reputation

What is the company's reputation among industry participants, customers, and in general? In what aspects is it highly or poorly regarded?

Industry: _____

Customers: _____

General: _____

F. Historical Strengths and Weaknesses

The competitor's principal strengths in these areas:

_____

_____

_____

The competitor's main weaknesses in these areas:

_____

_____

_____

COMPETITIVE ANALYSIS WORKSHEET 17

ANALYSIS SHEET: PRODUCTS

Competitor name: _____

A. Product Lines

List the company's principal product lines in order of revenue contribution:

Product Line	Revenue Past Two Years 19__ 19__	Percent of Total Revenue	Percent of Total Operating Profit	Approx. Market Share
_____	____ ____	____	_____	_____
_____	____ ____	____	_____	_____

List the three main customers for each product line and the percent of the competitor's sales they account for:

Product Line	Customer #1	Share	Customer #2	Share	Customer #3	Share
_____	_____	____	_____	_____	_____	____
_____	_____	____	_____	_____	_____	____

B. Market Leadership

Are any of the company's products market leaders?   ____ Yes   ____ No

Which ones? _____

_____

How has the company attained leadership (marketing skill, low costs, etc.)?

_____

_____

C. Product Line Dimensions

The company is:

____ Full-line   ____ Niche-oriented

Are the company's product lines:

____ Deep   ____ Shallow

In what significant areas of the market does the company not participate?

_____

_____

D. Product Strategy

How would you describe the company's product strategy?

____ Unique products   ____ Differentiation   ____ Standardization

Explain how the company applies this strategy:

Product 1 _____ : _____

Product 2 _____ : _____

Product 3 _____ : _____

What are the company's main strengths in product line and strategy?

_____

_____

What are the company's main weaknesses in these areas?

_____

_____

E. Product Quality

Product	Quality Rating (High, Average, Low)	Major Defects
_____	_____	_____
_____	_____	_____

Overall, the company's quality reputation is:

___ High   ___ Medium   ___ Low

The trend in quality is:

___ Improving   ___ Static   ___ Worsening

Principal or significant quality problems: _____

_____

F. Service

Is service an important aspect of product strategy?   ___ Yes   ___ No

Is service a source of revenues?   ___ Yes   ___ No

How is service sold (e.g., service contracts)? _____

Is the price of service bundled into product price?   ___ Yes   ___ No

What is the emphasis of service?

___ Presale   ___ Installation

___ Maintenance   ___ Repair

How is the service function structured (e.g., company's technicians, independent service specialists, etc.)?

_____

_____

What are the company's strengths in quality and service?

_____

_____

_____

What are the company's weaknesses in these areas?

_____

_____

_____

G. Product Development

List all the new products the company has introduced in the past two years:

	Still on the Market		
Product	Yes	No	Market Share
_____	____	____	_____
_____	____	____	_____
_____	____	____	_____

What is the company's general product development strategy?

___ Leader   ___ Follower   ___ Applications

If a follower, does the firm follow quickly with its own product or wait until the leader's product is established?

_____

_____

H. Research

Which methods does the company use for research?

___ Internal R&D department   ___ Independent lab

___ Licensing   ___ Joint Ventures

___ Other: _____

The company's research efforts are: ___ Centralized   ___ Decentralized

What is the technical focus of its research (e.g., electronics, mechanical design, etc.)?

_____

How many patents has the company taken out in the past two years? _____

Technical areas the patents concern: _____

List the firm's research facilities:

Facility _____ Area of Research _____

_____   _____

_____   _____

_____   _____

How does the company fund R&D (central budget, business unit budget, etc.)?

_____

Research spending past three years:

	Amount	Percent of Operating Profits
19____	_____	_____
19____	_____	_____
19____	_____	_____

What managers in the company approve research spending?

_____

List the company's strength in product development and research:

_____

_____

_____

List the company's weaknesses in this area:

_____

_____

COMPETITIVE ANALYSIS WORKSHEET 18

ANALYSIS SHEET: MARKETING

A. Overview

How would you rate the company's general marketing skills?

_____ Excellent _____ Good _____ Fair _____ Poor

Does it make use of market research? _____ Yes _____ No

Does it respond well to customers' needs? _____ Yes _____ No

How important are key customers?

_____ Crucial _____ Important _____ Not Important

What brand names does the company use? _____

_____

How valuable are these brand names?

_____ Very _____ Somewhat _____ Not Very

Describe the competitor's main marketing strengths:

_____

_____

_____

Describe the competitor's main weaknesses:

_____

_____

_____

B. Promotion

	Competitor	Industry Average
Total promotional spending during latest year	_____	_____
Ratio of promotional spending to sales	_____	_____

How effective is the general image of the company through its promotional activity?

_____

_____

_____

What promotional spending does the firm devote to:

Advertising	_____ percent	Trade promotions	_____ percent
Coupons	_____ percent	Direct main	_____ percent
In-store	_____ percent	Other _____	_____ percent

What advertising agency does the company use? _____

How strong is this agency in this field?

_____ Strong   _____ Average   _____ Weak

How would you rate the company's skill in:

	Excellent	Good	Fair	Poor
Advertising	_____	_____	_____	_____
Media selection	_____	_____	_____	_____
Point-of-purchase display	_____	_____	_____	_____
Sales literature/brochures	_____	_____	_____	_____
Trade shows, exhibitions	_____	_____	_____	_____
Other marketing areas:				
_____	_____	_____	_____	_____
_____	_____	_____	_____	_____
_____	_____	_____	_____	_____
_____	_____	_____	_____	_____

What patterns are apparent in the firm's promotional activity:

_____ Sporadic   _____ Long-term continuity   _____ Seasonal

_____ Focused on product introductions   _____ Opportunistic

Describe the company's strengths in promotion:

_____

_____

_____

Describe the company's weaknesses in this area:

_____

_____

_____

C. Distribution

Which distribution channels does the company use?

_____

Which channels does it not use?

_____

How many intermediaries are there between the company and its ultimate customers?

_____

List the intermediaries:

Intermediary	Geographic Scope	Generalist/ Specialist	Full Line/ Partial	Company	Franchise	Independent
_____	_____	_____	_____	_____	_____	_____
_____	_____	_____	_____	_____	_____	_____

How are the company's relations with intermediaries?

____ Excellent ____ Good ____ Fair ____ Poor

How important is the company's business to its top three intermediaries?

	Crucial	Important	Insignificant
1. _____	_____	_____	_____
2. _____	_____	_____	_____
3. _____	_____	_____	_____

What are the main advantages of the competitor's distribution system?

_____

What are the main disadvantages?

_____

D. Sales

Does the company use its own sales force?   ____ Yes   ____ No

Number of sales representatives: _____

What areas (geographic, market segments) are covered by direct sales?

_____

What is the general background of the company's salespeople (sales, technical, production, etc.)?

_____

How would you rate the company's training of salespeople?

____ Excellent   ____ Good   ____ Fair   ____ Poor

How is the sales force organized?

____ Geographic   ____ Customer groups

____ Product line   ____ Centralized

____ Applications   ____ Decentralized

What compensation arrangement does the company have with sales representatives?

___ Straight commission   ___ Bonus plan

___ Commission + salary   ___ Profit sharing

___ Other: _____

What does the commission/bonus depend on?

___ Volume   ___ Market share   ___ Margin   ___ Other ___

What sales strengths does the company possess?

_____

_____

_____

What sales weaknesses has it shown?

_____

_____

_____

COMPETITIVE ANALYSIS WORKSHEET 19

ANALYSIS SHEET: PRICING

A. Position

How would you describe the competitor's general price positions?

___ High   ___ Average   ___ Low   ___ Mixed

Has this position changed in the past three years?   ___ Yes   ___ No

Explain:

_____

B. Strategy

This competitor's pricing strategy is best described as:

       ___ Total cost pricing   ___ Value pricing

       ___ Capacity pricing   ___ Learning curve pricing

       ___ A mixture of strategies

Has the strategy been successful?   ___ Yes   ___ No

Explain:

_____

_____

C. Tactics

How many of these terms describe the competitor's approach to pricing tactics:

       ___ Price leader   ___ Aggressive   ___ Quick follower

       ___ Slow follower   ___ Defensive   ___ Consistent

       ___ Erratic

Does the competitor use frequent price changes?   ___ Yes   ___ No

If yes, why? _____

How do the following figure into pricing tactics?

Credit terms _____

Service _____

Warranties/guarantees _____

Financing _____

Terms of sale _____

Who controls the competitor's pricing?

	Influence			
	Much	Some	Little	None
Top management	____	____	____	____
Division/plant managers	____	____	____	____
Sales managers	____	____	____	____
Financial managers	____	____	____	____
Sales representatives	____	____	____	____

How does the competitor use discounts?

____ Quality   ____ Inventory reduction

____ Product introductions   ____ Competitive countermoves

____ Slow sales   ____ Key customers

____ Other: _____

What are the competitor's main strengths in pricing?

_____

_____

_____

What are the competitor's main weaknesses in pricing?

_____

_____

_____

COMPETITIVE ANALYSIS WORKSHEET 20

ANALYSIS SHEET: PRODUCTION

A. Vital Statistics

Plant: _____ Location: _____

Products: Capacity per month:

_____ _____

_____ _____

_____ _____

Year plant built: _____ Year modernized: _____

Book value: _____ Replacement value: _____

Work force: Shift 1 _____ Shift 2 _____ Shift 3 _____

Equipment:

Machine	Output per Day	Age	Comment
_____	_____	_____	_____
_____	_____	_____	_____
_____	_____	_____	_____

Advantages/disadvantages:

Feature	Advantage	Disadvantage	Notes
Shipping/receiving	_____	_____	_____
Available transportation	_____	_____	_____
Warehouse facilities	_____	_____	_____
Surrounding environment	_____	_____	_____
Energy supplies/costs	_____	_____	_____

Feature	Advantage	Disadvantage	Notes
Communication	_____	_____	_____
Pollution situation	_____	_____	_____
Plant safety	_____	_____	_____
Community relations	_____	_____	_____
Local government regulation	_____	_____	_____
Local business climate	_____	_____	_____
Other: _____	_____	_____	_____
_____	_____	_____	_____

B. Production Strategy

	This Year	Last Year	Five-Year Average	Goal
Production	_____	_____	_____	_____
Capacity	_____	_____	_____	_____
Utilization	_____	_____	_____	_____

Volatility of capacity utilization past five years:

Highest ____   Lowest ____   Average ____

Are production facilities flexible (e.g., can they be used to produce other products)?

____ Yes   ____ No

Explain: _____

How easy would it be for the competitor to add capacity?

____ Easy   ____ Difficult   ____ Requires new facility

Production facility/capacity advantages and disadvantages:

_____

_____

C. Supply

The general supply strategy of this company is:

———— Backward integration ———— Sourcing ———— Mixed strategy

Has the company made any significant make/buy decision in the past five years?

———— Yes ———— No

Explain: ————————————————————————————————

List the firm's three main suppliers:

Company   Material/Component Supplied

————————————————   ————————————————————

————————————————   ————————————————————

————————————————   ————————————————————

How are the company's relations with suppliers?

———— Stable/long-term ———— Erratic/short-term ———— Mixed

Are any of the materials/components the company buys in short supply?

———— Yes ———— No

Explain: ————————————————————————————————

Other supply problems, risks:

——

Competitor's main supply strengths:

————————————————————————————————— ————————

——

Competitor's main supply weaknesses:

——

——

D. Costs

General cost level compared to industry:

___ High   ___ Average   ___ Low

Cost goal: ___ High cost   ___ Average   ___ Low cost

Has the competitor employed formal cost-cutting programs during the past three years?

___ Yes   ___ No

Explain:

_____

How are the competitor's costs apportioned?

Materials:	___ percent	Administrative:	___ percent
Labor:	___ percent	Marketing/sales:	___ percent
Overhead:	___ percent	Other:	___ percent

What has the company's revenues per employee been during the past five years?

	Industry Average
19__ : _____	_____
19__ : _____	_____
19__ : _____	_____
19__ : _____	_____
19__ : _____	_____

Has the company employed any productivity improvement programs during the past three years?

___ Yes   ___ No

Explain:

_____

Competitor's cost strengths:

_____

_____

Competitor's cost weaknesses:

_____

_____

E. Additional Production Factors

Inventory past three years:

	19___	19___	19___
Average inventory	_____	_____	_____
Inventory turns/year	_____	_____	_____

How would you describe the company's inventory policy (e.g., attention to inventory management, attitude to stockouts, etc.)?

_____

_____

Other production advantages:

___ Work flow   ___ Automation   ___ Tooling

___ Material handling   ___ Change-over   ___ Other: _____

Overall production strengths:

_____

_____

_____

Overall production weaknesses:

_____

_____

_____

12

How to Evaluate Competitors' Administration and Finances

G athering information on the administrative and financial strengths
and weaknesses of your competitors is critical to your overall
analysis of their position in the industry, and the threat they pose to
you. Add this material to the Competitive Analysis Worksheets you
completed in Chapter 11 as you build up your Competitor Profile.

Personnel

Competitive Analysis Worksheet 21 covers the competitor company's
nonmanagement personnel. Because of the important contribution
that people make to the success of any enterprise, this factor de-
serves close attention.

Policy

Use Part A of Competitive Analysis Worksheet 21 to record general
data about the company's work force patterns and to evaluate its policy toward employees. Most companies' approaches fall into four
main categories:

Paternalistic. The company is protective of workers, reluctant to
resort to layoffs, pays adequate wages and benefits, and tries to
avoid conflicts, but does not include workers in decision making.
In some cases, the company guarantees its employees a job for
life. This is true with many Japanese firms.

Participative. These firms encourage input from employees into
decision making. They usually give workers opportunities to
exercise their initiative and encourage them to feel they have a
stake in the company.

Contractual. Here the firm's employee relations are determined
largely by union contracts. Work rules and wage agreements are
negotiated and adhered to. Relationships tend to be impersonal.

Hire/Fire. In this case, the company takes an opportunistic
approach to workers. No effort is made to establish long-term

loyalty. Employees are hired when work is available and laid off when business slows. Wage levels are usually low and morale may be poor.

The competitive implications of personnel policy depend on how well the policy works. A company with a contractual policy is guaranteed a certain stability, but may lack flexibility when quick changes in work force make-up are needed. A company that takes a hire/fire approach might be successful in keeping labor costs down. But perhaps its service will suffer, or it will be unable to recruit workers in order to take advantage of an opportunity.

Look at how the policy is working internally. For example, do employees abuse work rules? Is a participative policy really boosting worker morale, or does it lead to confusion and lack of discipline?

Next, take a general look at personnel relations. Are there any competitive weaknesses you can spot? Is the quality of the company's products suffering because of low morale? Has the competitor been unable to successfully increase productivity because of worker resistance? Are particular areas of the firm having labor problems?

Motivation/Morale

Part B of Competitive Analysis Worksheet 21 focuses on the motivation and morale of workers. Begin by looking at the means that the company uses to motivate workers. Does fear of reprimand or dismissal prompt workers on a day-to-day basis? If they are not afraid of punishment, are they working for specific, short-term rewards—as in a company that uses piecework? Is motivation left to the skill of individual supervisors? Is there a feeling of esprit de corps, of teamwork?

How accommodating is the company toward workers? How effective is management's motivation policy in maintaining worker morale? Are morale problems affecting production rates? Quality? Service? Any of these factors may provide competitive openings for your own company.

. . . .

Information Key

Ask your personnel department to locate an employee of your company who formerly worked for the competitor. Ask his views on the following topics:

Motivation techniques: _____

Morale level: _____

Personnel relations problems: _____

_____

Turnover/absenteeism: _____

. . . .

What has been the competitor's level of turnover? Is there a particular type of worker that it has trouble holding onto? Does high turnover increase its training costs? Leave it with a less skilled work force? Has absenteeism affected its production?

Wages

Wage levels are an important cost factor, but they have other competitive implications as well. They can affect the quality of workers the competitor is able to hire, the stability of its work force, and the level of morale of its employees. Compare its general wage rates with the industry average. Take into account as well the local labor situation and pay levels.

The determining factor for pay raises is also important. Most companies use one or more of the following criteria:

1. **Longevity.** Builds long-term loyalty, reduces the impact of wage raises as a motivational incentive.

2. **Position.** Depends entirely on the job the employee is doing, provides an incentive to advance to higher-paying positions, limits flexibility in paying workers within a level.

Information Key

In order to focus on wage levels, list three employee categories and determine the wages paid by your company and by the competitor:

Position	Your Wage Per Hour	Competitor's Wage
_____	_____	_____
_____	_____	_____
_____	_____	_____

3. **Achievement.** Rewards the worker for particular contributions, encourages initiative, but can also create resentment and ill-will.

Each wage structure has its advantages and disadvantages. Think about what your competitor is trying to achieve and how successful its policy is.

Unionization

A major distinction relative to the competitor's costs, productivity, and flexibility is whether its plants are unionized. In Part D of Competitive Analysis Worksheet 21 list any unions and the workers they represent. Think about the company's relations with its unions. Is your competitor combative in negotiations with its workers' representatives? Could this cause competitive weaknesses in the future in the form of union intransigence? How has the union responded to the company? Has it recognized cost and operating difficulties and made concessions? Has it been suspicious of management motives? What has been the history of strikes and other job actions at your competitor's plants?

Work rules are a final aspect of union relations to consider. How much flexibility does your competitor have in directing its work force? How are work rules adding to its costs or diminishing productivity? Where are your advantages in these areas?

. . . .

Information Key

Imagine two employees beginning work at your company and at your competitor's plant as production workers. What kinds of orientation, indoctrination, training, early supervision, and so forth would each receive? How does this affect the long-term performance of each?

Your company   Competitor

_____   _____

_____   _____

_____   _____

_____   _____

. . . .

Recruiting and Training

The last personnel topic is how your competitor recruits and trains its workers. Competitively, the question is how quickly the company can add workers to increase production, the overall quality of its work force, and how well it trains workers. Part E of Competitive Analysis Worksheet 21 can be used to track a competitor's recruiting and training.

Does the competitor use any special advertising or other recruiting methods to attract hourly employees? Does the company ever have trouble finding the number of employees needed? Are some of its new employees less skillful or experienced than the firm would prefer? How selective is the company? Where does the competitor put its training emphasis? Are employees given thorough training before they begin work? Do they learn on the job? Does the company encourage them to continue to expand their skills?

Now consider all facets of the competitor's personnel policy and pinpoint its strengths and weaknesses. In general you should ask: Given the advantages of a skillful and stable work force, how do the competitor's policies bring this about or fail to do so? In what ways has the competitor been able to hold down labor costs without sacrificing morale or quality?

Key Executives

Competitive Analysis Worksheet 22 provides a form for profiling the key executives in the competitor company. Reproduce it and fill out a copy for the chief executive, the chief operating officer, and key staff executives such as the top financial officer. Focus on the real decision makers—in a sales-oriented company, the vice-president of sales; in a technology firm, the head of research and development.

Background

Part A of Competitive Analysis Worksheet 22 deals with the executive's background and experience. How has his training influenced his view of business? Has a background in accounting made him "numbers-oriented"? Has his education as a lawyer made him a shrewd negotiator? How has his work experience shaped him? Has he spent his career in his current industry, so that he knows the business thoroughly? Is he a newcomer who doesn't yet understand the subtleties of the market?

The type of companies that he has worked for will be a factor. Is he a "company man" who has spent his career with his current firm, working his way through the ranks? Is he used to the bureaucracy and leeway for error encountered in a large corporation?

How broad has the executive's experience been? Has he had hands-on operating experience? Or have his duties been limited to staff functions?

Executives will also be influenced by the major events they've experienced. A manager who has been through a cash-flow crisis or bankruptcy may tend to be financially conservative for the rest of his

. . . .

Information Key

List two executives from your own company whom you know well. Cite incidents from their background or work experience which have had an effect on the way they manage today:

Executive #1: _____

Incident/influence/effect: _____

Executive #2: _____

Incident/influence/effect: _____

. . . .

career. An executive who has overseen the introduction of a very successful product might emphasize research and development.

Management Style

During the early 1980s, U.S. auto companies were experiencing hard times and severe losses. Both Chrysler and American Motors faced bleak prospects. The approaches of the managements of the two companies differed, however. American Motors retrenched. It sold a greater interest in the company to Renault and cut the company's line of passenger cars to two models. Chrysler, led by chief executive Lee Iacocca, took a different route. Iacocca in effect "bet the company" on the 1983 model year. The corporation amassed large debts in order to cut costs and maintain a full line of products. If 1983 had proven to be a repeat of the previous two years, the company could well have gone bankrupt. Fortunately, auto sales turned up and Chrysler was able to make a profit.

This incident shows the major competitive influence that can be exerted by the management style of a company's executives. A manager who enjoys taking risks and is willing to "gamble" on a decision will be an entirely different type of competitor than the one who always looks for the "sure thing."

Special areas of interest or sets of values can also inform you about how a competitor might react. Figure 13 gives some profiles of executives, briefly relating their management style or backgrounds. Read these over, then try to sum up the executive's strengths and weaknesses.

EXECUTIVE PORTRAITS

1. *R. Gordon McGovern* had a reputation as a skillful marketer and an astute developer of successful new products. His career was spent mainly with Pepperidge Farms, Inc. which he turned into a highly successful and innovative baking company during his 12 years as president.

Pepperidge Farms was acquired by Campbell Soup. McGovern was appointed president of the parent firm four years later. Campbell was a successful but highly conservative company. It had not introduced a major new product line in 10 years. Under his leadership, Campbell became much more aggressive in its marketing and product development. Three completely new product areas were pioneered in the first years of McGovern's management. The marketing budget was increased by 25 percent.

The results: a new—but predictable—competitive situation.

2. *Donald V. Seibert* began his career at J.C. Penney in 1947 as a shoe salesman. He spent many years as store manager. Later he moved into the corporate ranks and served as director of planning.

What could competitors expect when Seibert took over as chairman in 1974? Having been a store manager, he increased the store managers' autonomy and input. Having spent so much time in the operating side of the business, he emphasized merchandising, upgrading the quality and image of Penney's products. His experience as a planner gave him a long-term, slightly cautious view of the company.

3. *John Sculley* served as president of PepsiCo's Pepsi-Cola USA division before becoming the chief of Apple Computer. What was the significance of a soft drink executive switching to a computer company?

His experience running a large consumer products company had given Sculley two strengths: marketing and strategy. He immediately applied both of them at his new job.

In strategy, he began to position the company as the only viable alternative to IBM in personal computers. In marketing, he applied innovative promotions and advertising to increase public awareness of Apple.

Figure 13. Reading between the Lines of Executive Portraits

Management Evaluation

Competitive Analysis Worksheet 23 gives you an opportunity to make a more general appraisal of the competitor's management. How capable are they? Are they, as a group, particularly aggressive? Lax? Competent? Impatient? Impulsive? Give your impressions of each level of management. Some companies, for example, have strong first-level managers but a weaker, bureaucratic group of middle managers. Top managers may be highly capable, but perhaps they haven't the strength in lower levels to carry out their plans. Fill in this information in Part A.

Management Development

Is the competitor aggressive in recruiting the top managerial candidates available? How much of an effort does the company make to recruit in colleges or to lure bright managers from other companies?

Also important is whether the company fills most of its management positions from inside or has to recruit senior managers from other companies. The latter may be an indication that the company's management development process is deficient. It may also have a negative effect on executive morale. How well does the competitor train and develop managers? Many management experts consider this a key indicator of the long-term health of the firm. Investigate the formal program the company uses to develop managers' skills and fill in Part B of Competitive Analysis Worksheet 23.

Management Changes

You should always be aware of any important management changes in your competitor's organization. Part C of Competitive Analysis Worksheet 23 looks at these changes and asks you to consider whether they are significant. They can mean that the competitor has been having trouble in certain areas, that it has decided to change directions, or both.

For example, Control Data recently demoted the head of its problem-ridden computer peripherals division and replaced him with an executive who had been running its financial services division. Competitors noted that while the new executive had little technical expertise, he has had success in improving profitability, doubling the financial services group's return on equity.

Compensation and Advancement

The compensation levels the firm offers can influence the quality of executives it recruits and its ability to retain them. Sometimes this information can have a direct competitive effect if managers from your company are moving to the competitor because of more attractive salary opportunities.

Also important are nonsalary forms of compensation. How great an incentive do they provide? Are they directly or indirectly related to the manager's performance? Some executive incentive programs have been criticized as focused on the short-term to the detriment of longer-term successes. Is this the case at your competitor's company? Are its executives' competitive reactions likely to be directed toward preserving short-term accomplishments?

Look as well at some of the other evaluation procedures in the company. Performance evaluation and management by objectives can have an effect on the way managers view their jobs and on their reactions to certain competitive situations.

How do managers win promotion? Is there a steady line of advancement through the ranks of management? Are promising younger executives promoted quickly? Can technical or sales managers achieve levels of status and compensation comparable to general managers without passing through the same executive positions? This "parallel track" approach is used by some firms to prevent skillful technical managers from having to leave their field in order to advance.

What about the company's executive succession? At some companies the process is very orderly. For example, at General Motors, the next president and chairman are sometimes known years before they take power. But at other firms the departure of a long-time chief executive may set off many months of turmoil, during which the company may be competitively vulnerable.

Finally, take time to sum up the company's management strengths and weaknesses. Think about managers both as individuals and as a team. In what areas are they especially capable? Finance? Production? Sales? In what areas do they display inadequacy? Marketing? Long-term strategy? Product development?

Administration and Organization

The way a company is organized can affect its ability to compete effectively. The basic question to look at here is how the company's organization meets the demands of its markets.

Structure

Part A of Competitive Analysis Worksheet 24 asks you to look at the company's structure. Which of the following seems to be the deciding factor in the company's structure:

1. **Function.** In this case the company relies on strong, centralized staff departments such as marketing, sales, finance, and product development.
2. **Markets.** Here, the company is organized in units that serve particular market segments. For example, it might have a unit that serves business customers, and another that deals with consumers.
3. **Product.** The company is divided according to product lines. Individual units may have their own marketing, R&D, and so forth, and may serve a variety of markets.

Most companies utilize a mixture of all three modes of organization. What you are looking for is the structural element that dominates the way the company competes.

. . . .

Action Probes

How can you use the greater flexibility of your executives to obtain a competitive advantage over rivals?

Does the chief executive of the competitor company have a particular "blind spot" that you can exploit through market tactics?

. . . .

For example, MCI, when it started in the communications business, was able to take business from AT&T partly because of the way in which it was organized. MCI was structured around markets, focusing on high-volume business customers. Its products and its functional setup were directed at serving this market. AT&T, on the other hand, was a full-line participant with fundamentally a functional organization. Its marketing department handled all the company's products and addressed a variety of markets. Its product development effort was centralized. As a result, MCI had a competitive advantage.

A combination structure works in some situations. For example, a company in the food service business served both business and institutional customers. In marketing, the company structured itself along market lines, with business units serving each customer group. But in other areas—research, finances, manufacturing—the firm decided that a functional setup was more efficient, so these areas were handled by centralized departments.

Always look at the advantages and disadvantages of a specific structure. For example, what advantages does a computer company obtain by structuring itself around product lines—mainframe computers, minicomputers, word processing equipment? What advantages does it obtain by using a market-oriented approach—systems for large businesses, for retail stores, for universities?

Authority

Part B of Competitive Analysis Worksheet 24 considers the alignment of authority in the company. Highly decentralized companies may be quick to respond to competitive challenges. But their reactions may

. . . .

Information Key

Draw up an organizational diagram for the competitor, showing as clearly as you can the lines of authority and the relative power of each manager. What does the chart reveal about the firm? Does it indicate any weaknesses or areas of possible confusion? Write your comments below:

_____

_____

_____

. . . .

not be as coordinated or as strong as those of a company where authority is concentrated at a central headquarters. A close study of the limits of authority of managers at various levels will give you a better way to anticipate the extent and speed of the company's reactions to your moves in the market.

Look, too, at how the units relate to the corporation. Do top executives overrule the decisions of division heads? Are a unit's profits funneled directly back to the corporate treasury?

What does the creation of new units signify? Chrysler recently set up an International Business Development group whose purpose is to investigate joint ventures overseas. Competitors can see in this an attempt by Chrysler to find less costly sources of components in foreign markets and perhaps to expand its international sales as well.

The ranking of executives within the competitor company may also be revealing. If the top sales manager is an executive vice-president, it's an indication that sales is seen as crucial in that firm. In other companies, R&D or finance executives may hold high positions, indicating the predominance of those functions.

Decision Making

Record information about decision making within the company in Part C of Competitive Analysis Worksheet 24. Are most decisions left up to

Action Probes

How can you make use of delay or confusion in the competitor's deci-sion-making system? For example, would a series of conflicting market signals particularly impede the firm's ability to react to actual events?

Are the competitor's reactions so predictable because of its inflexible de-cision-making system that you can preplan a counterattack to the firm's response to one of your moves in the market?

· ·

line managers? Or do central committees become involved even in day-to-day details? Does one functional department have a say in a large proportion of decisions? For example, does the financial depart-ment sometimes veto operating plans?

Is the company an autocracy, with decisions and orders flowing downward from the chief executive or other top managers? Or does the firm look for a wide consensus before decisions are made? You need to get an idea of the decision-making process before you can begin to speculate about the direction and strategies the company might adopt.

Part C of Competitive Analysis Worksheet 24 also asks you to look at the extent to which bureaucracy affects the company. Is the firm slow to react because initiative becomes entangled in red tape? How fast does the competitor make important decisions? Once decided, are plans carried through forcefully? Or does the company often change direction later?

What about the company's controls? Do overly rigid controls make the competitor's reactions inflexible? Fill in the information about the com-pany's board of directors. In some firms, the board has a great deal of say about strategic direction, and may even become involved in day-to-day operating decisions. In others, it has almost no influence on the company's affairs.

Look at other influences on decisions as well. For example, the annual business plan of Eastern Air Lines had to be approved by its major lenders when the company was in technical default of its loan agree-ments. Former executives (e.g., Harold Geneen at ITT or William Paley at CBS) may retain a great deal of influence in the company long after they have retired. Both those men are widely held responsible for the removal of successor chief executives. Foundations, families, and governments can all play a part in influencing a competitor's decisions.

Finally, consider the strengths and weaknesses of the company's structure and organization. Think about the way your company is organized. Where do you have an advantage? Which company serves its market better? Which is more flexible? Which is quicker in making decisions?

Finances

A company's financial sphere holds two areas of particular competitive interest: trends and capabilities. More important than a comparison of absolute profitability, for example, is a look at how the competitor's level of profits is changing.

Capabilities refer to the firm's ability to acquire and pay for capital. Can the company acquire financing quickly to build a plant and take advantage of a competitive opportunity? Or is the firm having a difficult time paying the interest on its current debt? These are important competitive considerations. Competitive Analysis Worksheet 25 will help you focus on them. Note that finances is a difficult area to research when your competition is composed of small or privately held firms. Adapt this Worksheet to your particular requirements.

Earnings

Part A gives an overview of the competitor's earnings and allows you to spot trends during the past three years. Comparing its levels to the industry average will put them in perspective. Keep in mind that the Worksheet is only meant to provide a summary. You will want to study the competitor's full income statements if they are available.

. . . .

Information Key

Suppose that the competitor was faced with important decisions in the following three competitive areas. At what level would the decision be made, who would make it, and how quickly would it be made?

1. A major pricing change: _____

_____

_____

2. A product extension: _____

_____

_____

3. A change in the number of shifts worked: _____

_____

_____

. . . .

Again, look for trends. Are earnings improving? Is the company increasing its operating margin? Does the firm tend to follow industry profitability cycles closely? How volatile are the company's earnings? Do they fluctuate from year to year? What competitive implications can you draw from the firm's earnings picture?

Pay attention to the quality of earnings. Some companies understate or overstate their earnings through accounting techniques. Extraordinary earnings or expenses can also complicate the picture.

A Competitive Analysis Source

Robert Morris Associates (Philadelphia National Bank Bldg., Philadelphia, PA 19107) puts out composite financial statements broken down by product classifications called *Annual Statement Studies.* Obtain these or similar industry averages and construct comparison statements for the competitor. Look for drastic differences and seek explanations.

. . . .

Action Probes

If the competitor's working capital resources are strained, might this be a good time for you to extend the credit you offer to customers in order to increase your market share?

How can you cut your own working capital needs in order to operate more efficiently and improve cash flow?

. . . .

Cash Flow

Part B of Competitive Analysis Worksheet 25 covers cash flow. This aspect of the competitor's finances may be even more important than earnings. If the firm does not have the cash to carry out competitive plans, it will be at a definite disadvantage. Even a profitable company can be affected by cash-flow problems that result in missed or late deliveries, disproportionate backlogs of orders, pressure from creditors, and operating problems. These difficulties may represent important competitive openings for you.

Look especially at these components of working capital:

Inventories. Are they growing faster than sales? Why? Will the company have to cut prices to clear overstocks? Have they made unwise purchasing decisions?

Accounts Receivable. If they are increasing as a percent of sales, is the company extending credit to customers who are a poor risk? Has the company extended their credit terms in order to attract more customers? How will this affect the competitive balance?

Accounts Payable. Is the company having trouble paying its bills? Has it negotiated more favorable terms for paying suppliers?

Look for specific cash-flow problems. When is the competitor typically short of cash? It may be vulnerable to competitive moves at this time. How closely does the firm monitor its cash flow? Some companies are sales-oriented and run into difficulties because they don't calculate the cash-flow effects of sales increases.

Finally, sum up the company's strengths and weaknesses in terms of earnings and cash flow. Is the firm consistently profitable? Does it have a great deal of "cushion" in its operating margin which will allow it to meet price challenges or expand into new markets? Are its cash resources already spread so thin meeting necessary expenses that it will be vulnerable to moves which cut into its share?

Capital

Part C of Competitive Analysis Worksheet 25 is concerned with the competitor's capital structure. The relationship of a company's debt to its total capital depends to a large extent on the common situation in the industry. Real estate companies, for example, are usually highly leveraged. Traditional manufacturing firms may have no debt at all.

Look at the sources of the firm's capital. If the company has internal sources, how are they used? For example, General Mills follows a common practice in transferring the cash generated by a mature product—its Gold Medal flour—into a growth business—its Red Lobster restaurant chain. Companies competing against General Mills in the restaurant business have to note this fact and analyze it when considering the company's ability to compete.

Has the company raised capital internally? Beatrice recently sold its chemical division, its food services business, and a liquor distributor subsidiary in order to pay off part of its $2.8 billion long-term debt. Keep an eye out for such moves of capital. They can be very revealing of the competitor's long-term strategy.

Key Ratios

Ratios are good for summarizing complex financial information. They also provide a convenient way to spot trends and compare one company against another. The four ratios in Figure 14 provide a good cross-sectional view of a competitor's finances. Use them for Part D of Competitive Analysis Worksheet 25.

COMMON FINANCIAL RATIOS

The *current ratio* is the most common measure of a firm's liquidity. It is obtained by dividing current assets by current liabilities. For example, a current ratio of 1.5:1 means the company's current assets are equal to 1.5 times its liabilities. A current ratio of 2.0:1 was traditionally considered desirable for most companies, but efficient handling of receivables and inventories, and strict management of cash may allow a company to operate safely with a lower ratio.

The *Price-Cost Margin* is obtained from the following formula:

$$\text{PCM} = \frac{\text{Sales (less freight)} - \text{material costs} - \text{in-plant payroll}}{\text{Sales}}$$

In other words, the ratio measures the percentage of revenues which are available after paying basic costs, to cover marketing, overhead, research, taxes, interest, and profits. If a company's PCM is .25, then 25 cents of every sales dollar is available for these purposes. The higher the PCM, the more discretion the company has in areas like advertising and internally financed expansion.

Days Sales in Receivables is calculated by:

$$\text{Days Receivables} = \frac{\text{Average accounts receivable}}{\text{Net sales}} \times 365$$

This determines the average amount of time the firm's customers take paying their bills. It is a good measure of the company's ability to handle its working capital and cash. An increase in this ratio means a slowdown in cash flow and potential bad-debt problems.

Return on total assets is a general indicator of the company's return on investment. To find it, add interest expenses (net of taxes) back to net income and divide by the firm's total capital. A long-term increase in this ratio indicates the company is improving its efficiency in generating earnings from its assets. A long-term decline shows a lower rate of profitability.

Figure 14. *Key Competitive Financial Ratios*

Additional Financial Data

Part E of Competitive Analysis Worksheet 25 covers some further aspects of the company's financial situation. If the competitor is a multinational firm, does it repatriate earnings from foreign subsidiaries? Or are they reinvested in the local business? What currency problems

. . . .

Information Key

Many companies use a *hurdle rate* to evaluate internal investment decisions. This is the rate of return which an investment must generate in order to be minimally attractive to the firm. If you can discover this rate, it may be helpful in analyzing the firm's competitive moves. If you don't know the specific rate the company uses, try to estimate it based on investment behavior and current rates of return on assets.

_____

_____

_____

. . . .

has the competitor had? Exchange rates can have major competitive significance. In 1984–1985, many U.S. companies suffered the effects of the high value of dollars in relation to most other currencies. Foreign firms were able to undersell American competitors without cutting into their own profits.

Does the competitor have a long tradition of paying dividends? A cut in its dividend may be an indication of serious financial problems. Continued payment of dividends during periods of low profitability may strain its cash flow.

Financial restraints—such as loan provisions—impede the company's competitive maneuvering. They might provide you with an opportunity to gain in terms of market share or position.

The company's criteria for financial success are also indicative of the competitive course it might take. If revenue growth is important, the firm is likely to be a fierce competitor for market share. But if return on investment is the primary measure, the company's executives are going to carefully evaluate long-term return before entering new businesses or investing additional funds in current areas.

Finish by evaluating the competitor's overall strengths and weaknesses financially. Look for limitations—in its access or use of capital, in its willingness to invest funds. Look for trends—in the structure of its capital base, in its liquidity.

COMPETITIVE ANALYSIS WORKSHEET 21

ANALYSIS SHEET: PERSONNEL

A. Policy and Relations

How many employees work for the competitor? _____

Salaried: _____　　　　　Hourly: _____

Number hired during past year: _____

Number laid off/retired:　　　　_____

Net change in employment:　　　_____

How would you characterize the competitor's personnel policy?

____ Paternalistic　　　____ Hire/fire

____ Participative　　　____ Contractual

How good have personnel relations been overall during the past two years?

____ Excellent　　____ Good　　____ Poor　　____ Erratic

Explain: _____

Have there been significant changes in personnel relations during this period?

____ Yes　　____ No

Explain: _____

B. Motivation/Morale

What is the principal means the company uses to motivate workers?

____ Fear　　　　____ Reward/promotion

____ Persuasion　　____ Esprit de corps

____ Supervisory skill

How would you describe the current state of worker morale?

____ Excellent　　____ Good　　____ Poor　　____ Mixed

Explain: _____

What is the company's rate of employee turnover?

Latest year _____   Three-year average _____

Industry average _____

C. Wages

How do the company's wage levels compare with the industry average?

____ High   ____ Average   ____ Low

What is the basis for wage increases?

____ Longevity   ____ Achievement   ____ Position

D. Unionization

Is the company unionized?   ____ Yes   ____ No   ____ Partially

List the unions involved and the worker groups they represent:

Union _____   Workers _____

_____   _____

_____   _____

What has been the general condition of company/union relations during the past two years?

____ Cooperative   ____ Neutral   ____ Hostile

What is the union's attitude toward work rules?

____ Flexible   ____ Inflexible

Explain: _____

E. Worker Recruiting and Training

What is the company's usual method for recruiting and hiring workers?

Skilled: _____

Unskilled: _____

Availability of labor force in the competitor's area of operation:

___ Plentiful   ___ Erratic

___ Scarce   ___ Seasonal/cyclical

Overall quality of competitor's work force versus industry average:

___ High   ___ Average   ___ Low

Training emphasis for employees:

___ Orientation   ___ On-the-job training

___ Prejob instruction   ___ Classroom instruction

Workers are generally:

___ Well trained

___ Adequately trained

___ Poorly trained

Describe the principal strengths of the competitor's work force:

_____

_____

_____

_____

Describe its main weaknesses in this area:

_____

_____

_____

_____

COMPETITIVE ANALYSIS WORKSHEET 22

ANALYSIS SHEET: EXECUTIVE PROFILE

Name _____ Title _____

Age _____ Years in current position _____

Responsibilities _____

A. Background

Education and degrees _____

Work history (list companies, positions, years) _____

_____

_____

Years with current company: _____

Areas of experience:

Industries: _____

Size of companies: ____ Small ____ Medium ____ Large

Functional areas: _____

List any major events to which the executive was exposed during career:

_____

_____

List major successes and failures:

_____

_____

_____

_____

_____

_____

B. Management Style

Briefly describe management style:

_____

_____

_____

_____

What attitude does this executive take toward risk (e.g., cautious, calculating, adventurous)?

_____

_____

Describe any areas of special interest or particular values:

_____

_____

Executive's main strengths:

_____

_____

_____

Executive's main weaknesses:

_____

_____

_____

COMPETITIVE ANALYSIS WORKSHEET 23

ANALYSIS SHEET: MANAGEMENT EVALUATION

A. General Rating

How do you rate the overall capability of the company's managers?

____ Excellent   ____ Good   ____ Fair   ____ Poor

Is the company dominated by a particular type of manager?

____ Yes   ____ No

Explain: _____

_____

How do you rate the competence of the following management levels?

Foremen: _____

Supervisors: _____

Middle managers: _____

Top executives: _____

B. Management Development

Give details about the company's management recruitment practices:

_____

_____

_____

Are most non-entry-level positions in the company filled through promotions?

____ Yes   ____ No

If not, why not? _____

_____

What management development techniques does the company use?

____ On-the-job training   ____ Job rotation

____ University courses   ____ "Apprenticeship" to a senior manager

____ Nonuniversity courses

____ Company-operated training seminars   ____ Other (give details)

_____

How would you rate the company's success at developing capable managers?

____ Excellent   ____ Good   ____ Fair   ____ Poor

Describe any management development problems:

_____

_____

_____

_____

C. Management Changes

Have there been any significant management changes or realignments during the past two years? Explain.

_____

_____

Do these changes indicate a new direction or strategy? Explain.

_____

_____

Do these changes indicate operating problems within the company? Explain.

_____

_____

D. Compensation and Advancement

How does the salary level of this company's management compare to the industry average?

      ___ High   ___ Average   ___ Low

What other forms of compensation are awarded to managers?

    ___ Profit sharing   ___ Life insurance

    ___ Bonuses   ___ Perquisites (house, car, etc.)

    ___ Stock options

What does the additional compensation depend on?

    ___ Guaranteed   ___ General performance

    ___ ROI goals   ___ Return on assets controlled by manager

    ___ Stock price rise

    ___ Other   ___ Earnings growth/sales growth

            _____

Does the company have a formal performance evaluation process?

        ___ Yes   ___ No

Does the company use a management-by-objectives system?

        ___ Yes   ___ No

What is the company's promotion policy? _____

_____

_____

Does the company have a mandatory or traditional retirement age?

        ___ Yes, age ___   ___ No

Describe the company's procedure for choosing successors to its senior managers:

_____

_____

List the strengths of the company's managers and management system:

_____

_____

_____

List the weaknesses of the company's managers and management system:

_____

_____

_____

COMPETITIVE ANALYSIS WORKSHEET 24

ANALYSIS SHEET: ADMINISTRATION AND ORGANIZATION

A. Structure

What is the basic structural framework of the company?

____ Functional   ____ Market-oriented   ____ Product-oriented

____ Mixed (explain) _____

How effectively does this structure answer the needs of the company's markets, strategies, and competition?

_____

If the company is divided into divisions or business units, give details:

_____

B. Authority

Is authority in the company: ____ Centralized   ____ Decentralized

How much autonomy is exercised by line managers?

____ Complete   ____ Much   ____ Some   ____ None

Explain: _____

_____

In what way do units interact with corporate headquarters (strict reporting, budgetary control, etc.)?

_____

_____

How do business units interact with each other (e.g., arms length transactions, close cooperation, shared overhead, etc.)?

_____

_____

C. Decision Making

Which group of managers has the most influence on decisions?

_____ Line   _____ Staff

Is one functional area of management particularly influential in decision making, setting strategy, and so forth (e.g., marketing, financial)?

Which one(s): _____

How would you describe the decision-making process in the company (e.g., top down, grassroots, committee-oriented)?

_____

_____

_____

Is the company affected by bureaucracy and/or red tape? Explain.

_____

How quickly are decisions made?   _____ Rapidly   _____ Slowly

Does the company's management often reverse decisions?

_____ Yes   _____ No

What controls does the company use? (Give available details.)

Financial controls: _____

Management controls: _____

What is the composition of the company's board of directors?

Member	Position or Background

Is the board dominated by management?   _____ Yes   _____ No

How much influence does the board have on strategic decisions?

_____ A great deal   _____ Some   _____ Very little

Other influences on competitor decision making (e.g., former executives):

_____

_____

_____

What are the strengths of the company's organization?

_____

_____

_____

What are the weaknesses of the organization?

_____

_____

_____

COMPETITIVE ANALYSIS WORKSHEET 25

ANALYSIS SHEET: FINANCES

A. Earnings

	This Year (Estimate)	19__	19__
Revenues	_____	____	____
Operating income	_____	____	____
Gross return on sales (ROS)	_____	____	____
Industry average ROS	_____	____	____

During the past five years, what have been the company's trends regarding:

	Higher (Percentage Increase)	Stable	Lower (Percentage Decrease)
Revenues	_____	_____	_____
Operating income	_____	_____	_____
Expenses (as percentage of sales)	_____	_____	_____
Interest (as percentage of sales)	_____	_____	_____
Selling and administrative costs (as percentage of sales)	_____	_____	_____

Have there been any extraordinary events that have affected earnings in the past five years? Explain.

_____

How would you rate the quality of the company's earnings (e.g., price increases, inventory revaluations, inflated profits)?

_____

B. Working Capital/Cash Flow

	This Year (Estimate)	19__	19__
Net income	_____	____	____
Depreciation	_____	____	____
Cash from operations	_____	____	____
Change in accounts receivable	_____	____	____
Change in accounts payable	_____	____	____
Capital spending	_____	____	____
Short-term debt, net increase/decrease	_____	____	____
Total change in working capital	_____	____	____
Net increase/decrease in cash	_____	____	____
Cash, beginning of year	_____	____	____
Cash, end of year	_____	____	____

Does the company have significant seasonal fluctuations in cash availability or working capital?   Explain:

_____

Which segments of the competitor's business are net consumers or providers of cash?

Consumers   Providers

_____   _____

_____   _____

_____   _____

Has the company had any severe cash shortages in the past three years? Detail:

_____

_____

_____

How skillful is the company's management of its cash and cash flow?

___ Excellent   ___ Good   ___ Fair   ___ Poor

Major strengths in earnings, cash flow:

_____

_____

_____

Major weaknesses in these areas:

_____

_____

_____

C. Capital

	This Year (Estimate)	19__	19__
Long-term debt	_____	____	____
Shareholders' equity	_____	____	____
Debt-equity ratio	_____	____	____
Total capital	_____	____	____

Is this company highly leveraged compared with the industry average?

___ Yes   ___ No

What is the structure of the firm's capital?

	Percent of Capital		Percent of Capital
Initial equity	_____	Debentures	_____
Retained earnings	_____	Bonds	_____
Bank debt	_____	Other	_____

Describe the company's banking relationships:

____ Excellent ____ Good ____ Fair ____ Poor

What is the company's credit risk rating (if any)? _____

Is additional financing readily available? ____ Yes ____ No

If yes, from what source(s)? _____

Does the company use short-term financing or factoring regularly?

____ Yes ____ No

If yes, give details:

_____

_____

D. Key Ratios

	This Year (Estimate)	19__	19__
Current ratio	_____	____	____
Price-cost margin	_____	____	____
Days sales in receivables	_____	____	____
Return on total assets	_____	____	____

E. Additional Financial Data

Does the company repatriate international earnings?

____ Yes ____ No

Has the company experienced any significant currency translation effects during the past three years?

____ Yes ____ No

If yes, give details: _____

Is the company vulnerable to currency fluctuations?

____ Yes ____ No

If yes, in which businesses, countries: _____

What is the company's dividend policy? _____

Is the company under any specific financial restraints (e.g., provisions of loans, preferred stock dividends, etc.)?

_____ Yes   _____ No

If yes, give details: _____

What is the company's most important financial criterion of success (e.g., earnings growth, sales growth, return on equity, etc.)?

_____

Describe the company's overall financial strengths:

_____

_____

_____

Describe the company's overall financial weaknesses:

_____

_____

_____

13

Basing Your Counterattacks on Your Competitors' Strategies

Your conclusions about competitor strategy will be drawn from a huge amount of diverse information, including all the Worksheets you fill in. From this impression you will be able to develop a clear idea of the competitor's strategy.

The value of analyzing that strategy lies in the help it gives you in shaping your own.

Summarizing Competitors' Strategies

Your review of the Worksheets you've already filled out will give you some essential elements of the competitor's strategy that you can put together to develop a summary. These include:

Principal competitive advantages

Predominant strengths

Actions taken in the recent past that have the most significant long-term consequences

Apply these three elements, for example, to the case of the Onyx Corp., a hypothetical electronics firm that produces customized integrated circuits. If you were a competitor, a review of your analysis of Onyx would show:

1. The firm's competitive advantage is its product quality.
2. Its strengths are in its highly skilled technicians and its rigorous testing procedures, as well as its ability to work with customers in product development.
3. Onyx recently broke ground for a new R&D lab.

After considering these points, you might sum up the company's strategy as follows:

"Onyx is pursuing a specialized, high-end market segment involving low-volume, superior quality production and technically advanced products."

. . . .

Information Key

List these three indicators of strategy to organize your thoughts on the exact definition of the strategy your competitor is following:

Key competitive advantage: _____

_____

_____

Principal strength: _____

_____

_____

Consequential recent action: _____

_____

_____

. . . .

This estimation of Onyx's strategy tells you a number of things. Onyx is unlikely to suddenly branch into high-volume, commodity circuit production (note the company is investing in a research facility, not production capacity). Service and quality will remain primary competitive arenas, not price or promotion. Proprietary technology may become a key competitive advantage.

Planning Your Own Reactions

How would you compete against Onyx? You might try to duplicate the capability of its circuits but offer them for a significantly lower price. Maybe you would invest in your own product development to try to come up with more attractive technological innovations. Or perhaps you'd target a slightly different customer segment. In any case, your study of the competitor's strategy will give you a better idea of how the market battle can be fought—and won.

Record your thoughts on strategy in Part A of Competitive Analysis Worksheet 26 at the end of this chapter. It is also worthwhile to look backward to try to determine the company's previous strategy. Has it been consistent? Has the strategy evolved? Does a pattern of vacillation indicate probable future changes? This will give you a clue to the certainty of your predictions.

How does the competitor company see itself? Does it consider itself a market leader—as companies like IBM, General Electric, and Procter & Gamble do? Is it an industry maverick, such as Federal Express was in parcel delivery or Iowa Beef Processors in meat? Does it see itself as a follower of industry trends? Is it an innovator? Figure 15 provides a brief view of strategic positioning.

Take into consideration the temporal focus of the company. Richardson-Merrell, a large pharmaceutical producer, for example, does not engage in long-range planning because it considers its markets too volatile. Some large manufacturing firms, on the other hand, routinely look 10 or more years into the future.

Whether the responsibility for planning strategy has been assigned to a particular department or manager is important, too. If not, strategic thinking in the company may be haphazard and unfocused. Try to pinpoint how and by whom strategy is set.

Weighing Competitive Commitment

Part B of Competitive Analysis Worksheet 26 looks at the competitor's commitment to various sectors of its company. Consider the following factors in weighing commitment:

History

Sector growth

Proportion of sales and profits from sector

Emotional attachment to sector

Total assets in sector

Recent investments in sector

Personnel assigned to sector

· ·

Information Key

Write a succinct definition of your own company's strategy in order to focus your thinking in this area:

_____

_____

_____

· ·

STRATEGY: A VIEW FROM THE INSIDE

More and more companies are formulating specific strategies in order to more effectively deal with future events. Here is what a few companies say about their own strategies.

Burndy Corp. (electrical connector producer, $232 million sales): "We are committed to being among the leaders in our industry as measured by sales growth and profitability, and toward that end have committed ourselves to a steady, dependable, and predictable performance improvement built on human, technological, and financial strengths."

Illinois Tool Works, Inc. ($592 million maker of specialty industrial systems and mechanical products): "Our key strategies, which remain unchanged and central to our business, are:

Build on our core businesses which are fasteners, components, packaging, electronics, specialty chemicals, instruments, tools, and gearing

Bring new products to known markets and/or current products to new markets

Maintain small, autonomous, and decentralized operations

Maintain a strong balance sheet to allow us to capitalize on opportunities as they arise."

General Electric ($27 billion diversified company): "General Electric formulated a strategy to become the most competitive enterprise in the world by being number one or number two in market share in every business we are in."

Figure 15. Actual Company Strategy Remarks

··

Action Probes

Can you take actions to encourage or facilitate the competitor leaving market areas where his commitment is low?

How has a commitment to a less attractive sector damaged the competitor or left him vulnerable?

··

Commitment determines many competitive reactions—both wise and unwise. AT&T, for example, is committed to remaining a factor in the telephone equipment business. Many new competitors have moved into this field in recent years, but all have to be aware that AT&T will put up a determined fight to remain a large factor in the field.

Control Data, on the other hand, was long committed to the computer time-sharing business because of the hefty profits the firm had traditionally made in that sector. But this commitment caused the firm to invest in time-sharing even after the business was hit by slow growth with the advent of the personal computer. The sector became a profit drain for Control Data.

Making Assumptions

Another area that will influence strategy and the way the company competes in the market is its assumptions. Fill in the assumptions that the competitor's managers are making about various facets of their business in Part C of Competitive Analysis Worksheet 26.

All strategic decisions rest on assumptions. A company makes a capital investment in production capacity because it assumes the market for its products will increase. It develops new products because it assumes a market need. MCI started up its long-distance phone business because it assumed that government regulators would allow it to compete as a common carrier along with AT&T, which then had a monopoly.

Matching Tactics to Execution

A company may have a valid strategy, but fail in the execution of it because its tactics are inconsistent with what it is trying to accomplish.

Hewlett-Packard's strategy in the electronic calculator market, for example, is to dominate the high-end, scientific segment. Its tactics: to develop technically advanced products, to keep in close touch with the needs of specific customer groups, to assure high quality performance. Since the tactics are consistent with its strategy, the firm has been successful.

Texas Instruments competes in the calculator market, but uses a different strategy. It produces dependable but lower-cost products on a mass basis. This goes along with its idea of being a price leader in the field, not a technology leader.

The New Process Co. is a catalog firm that pursues a strategy of selling to the low-end segment of the mail-order market. Its tactics include a highly automated order-processing facility to keep costs down and a conservative line of merchandise. These tactics fit its strategy—they're consistent.

Record your impressions about the consistency of the competitor's strategy and tactics in Part D of Competitive Analysis Worksheet 26.

Action and Reaction to Competitive Moves

The next area to look at is the actual competitive struggle. Begin by considering how the company reacts to competitive maneuvers. Is it primarily an aggressive or defensive firm? Is it quick or slow to react to important developments? Are its reactions usually well thought out, or do managers tend to be impulsive?

For example, you might introduce a process innovation that enables you to dramatically cut costs for a particular product. When you introduce a price decrease, you may expect your competitor, whose costs

. . . .

Information Key

List two of your own moves in the market recently and describe how the competitor reacted. Then list two specific competitive moves that the competitor has initiated and describe their effect:

Your move: _____

Competitor's reaction: _____

Your move: _____

Competitor's reaction: _____

Competitor's move: _____

Effect: _____

Competitor's move: _____

Effect: _____

. . . .

are higher, to leave that particular area of the market. Instead, it matches your price. Its move may not be rational, but simply an impulsive reaction to any price threat. If you haven't analyzed the company and foreseen this possibility, though, the move may disrupt your own plans. Fill out Part E of Competitive Analysis Worksheet 26.

Head-to-Head Competition

The final subject of Competitive Analysis Worksheet 26, in Part F, is a look at the competitor vis à vis your own company. How will its strategy affect you? What defensive moves or counterattacks will it require? For example, if the competitor's strategy is to aggressively increase market share and aim for low-price, high-volume production, does this mean you are likely to lose customers to it? Which ones? What can you do to prevent this loss of share? If you can't prevent it, can you specialize in more profitable segments or geographic areas?

Just as important is to recognize the opportunities that the competitor's strategy opens up for you. For example, perhaps the competitor company has decided to expand its product line in order to become a full-line producer. You may see that it is spreading its sales and promotion efforts too thinly. Your counterattack might be to focus on a few very profitable customer groups with intensive promotion and sales efforts of your own. This could help you increase your share and boost profits as well.

How does the competitor view your company? Do its managers follow your market moves closely? Is your market share so much smaller that your actions are ignored? Is the competitor so involved in a market war with another firm that it is unlikely to notice the actions of your company?

Sum up your overall evaluation of the company as a competitor. What threat does the company pose to you today in direct competition?

Finally, think about the competitor's strategic strengths and weaknesses. Consider its strategy, assumptions, consistency of its tactics to what it is trying to accomplish, and its past performance as a competitor. Is its strategy in line with what is actually happening in the market? Is it based on incorrect assumptions? Does the competitor have the resources to carry it out?

COMPETITIVE ANALYSIS WORKSHEET 26

ANALYSIS SHEET: COMPETITOR'S STRATEGY

A. General Strategy

Sum up briefly the competitor's strategy for success:

_____

_____

How has the company's strategy changed or evolved over the years?

_____

_____

How successful has the strategy been in the past?

____ Very successful ____ Moderately successful ____ Unsuccessful

Why is it likely to succeed or fail in the future?

_____

_____

Does the competitor focus primarily on the long- or short-term?

____ Long-term ____ Short-term ____ Both equally

Does the company have a strategic planning effort? ____ Yes ____ No

If yes, what person or committee is responsible for strategic decisions?

_____

_____

Describe the strategic planning process:

_____

_____

B. Commitment

List market segments, customer groups, products, geographic areas, or other logical divisions of the competitor's business. Rate each according to the management's commitment to remain in the sector and succeed:

Sector	High Commitment	Medium Commitment	Low Commitment	Seeking to Close/ Divest
_____	_____	_____	_____	_____
_____	_____	_____	_____	_____

C. Assumptions

Briefly describe the basic assumptions that the competitor's managers have made in the following area and used in their strategic formulations:

Market growth: _____

Market changes: _____

Technological developments: _____

Competition: _____

The competitor's own market position: _____

The environment (social, political, etc.): _____

Other: _____

_____

D. Consistency

What specific tactics has the competitor used or planned in order to accomplish the goals of its strategy?

_____

_____

How well do these tactics serve the goals of the strategy?

____ Excellent   ____ Good   ____ Fair   ____ Poor

Does the company have the internal capabilities (finances, management talent, etc.) to accomplish its strategy?

_____ Yes _____ No

Explain:

_____

Describe the major inconsistencies between the competitor's tactics and/or its capabilities and its strategic goals:

_____

_____

_____

E. Competition

Which of these terms describe the way the competitor usually reacts to direct competitive moves?

_____ Aggressively   _____ Preservation of status quo   _____ Slowly

_____ Quickly   _____ With careful planning   _____ Impulsively

_____ Defensively

What types of competitive challenges can the company best handle (e.g., advertising, price, new products, etc.)?

_____

_____

What types of challenges is it not prepared to handle?

_____

_____

F. Head-to-Head Competition

What specific effects is the competiror's strategy likely to have on our company if it succeeds?

_____

_____

What opportunities does the competitor's strategy leave open for us?

_____

_____

How does the competitor view our company?

_____

_____

The best overall rating of this company as a competitor is:

____ Definite threat   ____ Potential threat   ____ Marginal threat

____ Not a threat

Sum up the competitor's strategic strengths:

_____

_____

_____

Sum up the major strategic weaknesses:

_____

_____

_____

14

Putting Competitive Analysis to Work for You

K now your enemy—the first principle of all conflict, whether on the battlefield or in the marketplace. Competitive analysis has given you an in-depth awareness of your competitors. It has shown you their strengths and weaknesses. It has given you insights into their strategies and the ways they might act and react in your business.

Finding Your Competitors' Weak Points

"You may advance and be absolutely irresistible if you make for the enemy's weak points," said Sun Tzu, the renowned Chinese military theorist. This principle holds true in the business battles you engage in with competitors. Attacks against their strengths are difficult and often fruitless. Attacks that challenge their weak points are likely to succeed.

Take the case in which your main competitor's greatest strength is its sales force. You are concerned about its recent increase in market share and wish to regain some of the ground you've lost. One approach might be to strengthen your own sales force—lure more experienced reps, train them better, support them better in the field. But consider: Your competitor is already ahead of you in this area. As you improve your sales effort—at a cost—it can do the same, probably more easily. You are attacking its strong point, paying a high price, and perhaps accomplishing little.

A better approach: Begin with competitive analysis. Identify the competitor's weakness. Suppose several of its customers have complained of inadequate follow-up service. The competitor fails to provide aid when customers encounter start-up problems or maintenance difficulties with its products. Your tactic: Strengthen your service department. Bundle a service contract into your selling price. Introduce an effective promotional campaign featuring your company as "the service specialists." Now the competitor is on the defensive. It's being attacked where it's weak. It will either have to lose service-sensitive customers to you or begin an expensive effort to upgrade its service function.

Information Key

Knowing your own company as well as you do, you probably can pick out at least one area in which you are vulnerable to the competition. Briefly note this below. Now, rethink your entire analysis of your principal competitor and try to spot a similar weakness that makes that company vulnerable.

Your weakness: _____

Competitor's weakness: _____

Consistency Is the Key

You've already seen how inconsistencies undermine strategy. Look for places where your competitors have built incongruities into their plans. An effective business plan requires congruity between three elements:

Goals

Opportunities

Resources

For example, a company in the cement business might set the goal of being the nationwide leader in concrete block production. Even if the firm possessed the resources to do so, it is unlikely the plan would succeed. The reason: No opportunity exists to establish such a position. The business has few economies of scale, high transportation costs, and a need for local contacts in the fragmented construction industry. Smaller local and regional firms could take advantage of this inconsistency to easily thwart the company's attempt to achieve its goal.

Even combining forces with the enemy is an option. See Figure 16.

Use Competitive Analysis Worksheet 27 to reexamine your competitor's market strategy. For every strategic goal, look at whether a realistic opportunity exists and whether the competitor has the necessary

---

PEACEFUL COEXISTENCE: HOW TO LIVE WITH COMPETITORS

Your competitor analysis will show you many areas where you can success-fully beat the competition. You should bear in mind, though, that conflict is not the only relationship you can have with rivals. Sometimes co-existence is a better strategy.

1. Competitors can motivate your company. AT&T long fought to preserve its monopoly in U.S. long-distance phone service and telephone equip-ment sales. Challenges by aggressive firms eventually opened a new era of competition. AT&T has become a more innovative and respon-sive company and was spurred to investigate many related business opportunities.

2. Competitors can establish entry barriers. The market share struggle among the few large cigarette companies in the United States is fierce. But their large marketing budgets are, together, an effective barrier to smaller firms trying to grab lucrative market segments. The promotional spending needed to overcome the barrier presented by the competi-tors together discourages new and disruptive entrants.

3. Competitors often share the cost of market development. They can make a product category more popular, improve the image of the prod-uct or industry, or standardize technology so as to exclude other com-petitors.

Remember that marketplace battles must have a clearly defined purpose. Bausch & Lomb fought hard against smaller competitors in the contact lens market. But instead of improving its ultimate position, it drove many smaller companies—which might have served specialty segments without harm to Bausch & Lomb—to be acquired by large, well-financed firms who wished to stake out a large position in the business. Ultimately, Bausch & Lomb faced stiffer competition than it would have if it had followed a policy of coexistence.

Figure 16. Combining Forces with the Enemy

resources to carry out the plan. Pinpoint inconsistencies and keep them in mind as you focus on weaknesses and plan your own strate-gies.

Management Posture

An old adage claims that battles are won not on the battlefield, but in the minds of the commanders. There have been many cases in which inferior forces have defeated superior opponents because of adroit strategy and tactical moves by one commander, faulty thinking by another.

Take the case in which you have decided that the managers of a competing firm are overly conservative. It has been a market leader for too long. Your tactic: Develop a new distribution technique—perhaps a new way of packaging your product that allows you to more easily give discounts for high volume. You offer that discount to volume purchasers. You know the competitor could match your price in order to retain its customers, but you rely on complacency. Your competitive analysis pays off—it is skeptical about your ability to hold your price. By the time it reacts, you've made a healthy gain in market share.

There are many examples of this use of competitor analysis to spot weaknesses in rival companies' management postures.

Large steel companies were complacent and this allowed competitors to set up minimills that attacked the big companies at their weak points—high overhead and lack of responsiveness to customers. The big mills were slow to react, and competitors gained in market share.

Product Weaknesses

Try to find weaknesses that are inherent in the competitor's product. Does it have defects that you can exploit? Is it outdated? Does it rely on obsolete technology? Is it easily copied? Can it be improved?

For example, in the early 1980s, the small firm Minnitonka introduced liquid hand soap in a pump dispenser. The item was extremely popular and Minnitonka's sales climbed from $25 million to $73 million in one year.

The product had a weakness, though. Since it had no proprietary aspects, it could be duplicated by any other manufacturer. Its very success encouraged 50 other companies, many with greater resources than Minnitonka, to enter the field. Minnitonka's sales growth was stopped cold.

· ·

Information Key

Take another look at your evaluation of the competitor's management. Does the background, experience, and past performance of the firm's top executives suggest any areas in which they are:

Predictable: _____

Complacent: _____

Neglectful: _____

· ·

A different but related problem arose at Xerox. Its product line was successful but interrelated. Xerox offered a series of increasingly more sophisticated copiers at prices which were structured to create a pattern of diminishing per-copy prices.

IBM introduced a copier that competed directly with Xerox's middle-level products and offered a price advantage. While Xerox could match the price, the fact that its price structure was interrelated meant that the company had to lower prices for *all* its machines in order to retain the logical structure. This is a classic example of using a weak point to gain a competitive advantage.

Perhaps product quality is an important factor in your industry. Is your competitor substituting cheaper materials in order to obtain a larger margin? Could this be a weak point?

Electronic controls have become a desirable feature of large appliances. Maytag has been slow to adopt this innovation, taking a wait-and-see attitude. General Electric, on the other hand, has made them a feature of its advertisements—hitting Maytag in a potentially weak spot.

Competing with Procter & Gamble: Finding Weaknesses in a Market Strongman

Procter & Gamble has long been considered one of the strongest marketing companies in the world. Companies wishing to do battle with it have had to find chinks in the firm's armor—its weak points. Here are some tactics they've employed:

. . . .

Action Probes

What is the single most common customer complaint about your main rival? How does this point to a weakness that you could exploit?

Is there a way you can change the "rules of the game" in order to turn a competitor's strength into a weakness (e.g., by making price a more important competitive factor if the competitor relies on high quality)?

. . . .

Product Benefits. While Procter & Gamble has always developed strong and innovative products, it hasn't always maximized the benefits to the consumer. Colgate-Palmolive was able to make significant inroads into Procter & Gamble's share of the toothpaste market by introducing a pump dispenser.

Areas Ignored. Sometimes, Procter & Gamble has ignored market sectors, leaving competitive openings. Thinking its laundry powders superior to any liquid, it failed to enter the liquid detergent market for many years. As a result, Lever Brothers' Wisk attained dominance in a substantial market segment.

Brand Confusion. Kimberly-Clark has continued to erode Procter & Gamble's lead in disposable diapers as Procter & Gamble attempts to compete with two premium-priced brands (Pampers and Luvs) instead of clearly differentiating the two.

Competitive Analysis Becomes Effective Action

You've been examining your competitor's weak points in order to employ an indirect approach in your competitive actions. Success will come from pitting your strength against a competitor's weakness, not from meeting its strength head on.

The reason for this approach is the same in business as it is in warfare—defense is easier than offense. In the marketplace, it is harder to win new customers, enter new markets, or expand your business than it is to hold customers and defend your market share.

Here are some of the ways you can exploit the competitor's weak points once you've identified them.

Flank Attack

This is the clearest case of using the indirect approach to attack weak points. An army is strong on its front, weak on its flanks. To conduct a flank attack, you must concentrate your own forces and attack the competitor from an angle.

Take the case of Super Value Stores, an innovative company which has become one of the largest grocery concerns in the United States. The company's managers, in devising their successful growth plans, have chosen not to attack established supermarket chains directly.

Instead, they've concentrated on their own strengths, which they define as extremely efficient warehouse operations and an ability to direct the efforts of independent supermarket owners. They've used these strengths to attack the chains' weakness: their centralization and corporate overhead.

Super Value provides advice, site selection, financing help, training, planning assistance, accounting, and other services to their 2,300 independent affiliates, making their stores better run than those of most independents. They provide efficient volume purchasing and supply, giving the stores a cost advantage over both independents and chain stores. The result: an enhanced ability to compete that has paid off in both growth and profit.

Honeywell, in devising its early strategies for marketing computers, noted that market leader IBM was making its strongest efforts in large cities where the concentration of customers was highest. To avoid attacking IBM at its strong point, Honeywell focused its sales and marketing efforts in smaller cities and was able to establish itself in the industry.

Riunite became the leading imported wine in the United States by carefully avoiding the strengths of other imports: the appeal of their high-class image and a taste that was favored by sophisticated wine

. . . .

Action Probes

Do you have plans currently on the drawing board which might have a better chance of competitive success if you speed their introduction?

What potential competitive moves of your rivals—that you have uncovered through competitor analysis—could you thwart by quickly moving to counter them?

. . . .

drinkers. Riunite aimed its strong marketing effort at a segment that other importers were ignoring—unsophisticated customers attracted by a more informal image. The result: a very rapid gain in market share.

Mobility

"I may lose a battle," Napoleon once remarked, "but I shall never lose a minute." He introduced the tactic of marching his troops at 120 paces per minute instead of the traditional 70. As a result, he won many battles through mobility instead of sheer force.

Procter & Gamble was testing a product innovation—resealable tabs—on its Pampers disposable diapers. Rival Kimberly-Clark assumed the new style would be popular, did little testing, and rushed its product to market. This allowed the firm to make inroads into Procter & Gamble's market share.

A company called Air Cruises, Inc. asked the government to approve a new inflatable life raft for airliners. While the product was being examined, two rival firms, through keen competitor information gathering, learned the details of the product. They developed competing rafts and Air Cruises was shut out of some markets before it even began to sell.

Direct Attack

Despite the general advice to avoid the direct approach, some firms have been successful in meeting a competitor head-on. Before you commence a direct attack, though, keep in mind that you need superior forces—in other words, it will be expensive. Also remember that you can still use indirect tactics, such as relying more heavily on particular market segments.

Coca-Cola, for example, used a direct approach when it attacked rival diet soft drink makers with its Diet Coke brand. The only indirect aspect of its approach was its use of a taste theme in its advertising, in contrast to the more typical low-calorie theme of other diet drinks. The campaign was both successful and costly. Coca-Cola employed a massive advertising budget and diluted its Coke trademark for the first time. But it was able to overwhelm its competitors and quickly establish Diet Coke as the largest selling diet soft drink.

Encirclement: Scripto's Thrust in Lighters

One variation of direct attack is to try to succeed by attacking on so many fronts that the competitor has to spread its defensive resources too thin. Eventually your attack can't be held off and you encircle the competitor's overextended lines.

This approach is being attempted by Tokai Seiki Co., the world's largest maker of cigarette lighters, in its attempt to wrest leadership of the U.S. market from Bic. Because of the strength of its resources, the firm is trying an all-out attack through its U.S. subsidiary Scripto. The goal: market leadership by 1987.

Currently, Bic holds 55 percent of the market and has already defeated Gillette in this area—the latter withdrew its Cricket product. Scripto's share today is 24 percent.

Here are some of the broad-based tactics that Scripto plans:

Price. Scripto plans severe price cutting during the introductory phase of the campaign, with four lighters offered for $1 and 20 million coupons distributed.

Personnel. Scripto has recruited Jack Paige, former marketing vice-president at Bic.

Segment Strategy. Scripto is confronting Bic's single product with three products differentiated by price and features.

Sales and Distribution. Scripto is trying to counter Bic's lead in distribution by hiring 100 new merchandising reps and increasing its sales force by 60 percent.

The success of this approach remains to be determined. Bic, for example, has already addressed the segmentation challenge by planning a new miniature model that it thinks will appeal to women. Whatever the outcome, the case serves as an illustration of a broad-based, direct attack on a market leader.

Guerrilla Warfare

Not all gains are made through concentrated attacks. Sometimes it is better to disperse your forces and conduct a competitive campaign that hits opponents at various points, harasses them, keeps them off balance.

A good example of guerrilla warfare in market competition occurred in 1967. Formula 409, then produced by a small private company, held 50 percent of the spray cleaner market. Previously, the larger household-products companies had ignored this relatively small segment. But Procter & Gamble decided to introduce a competing brand, called Cinch. Test marketing was scheduled for Denver.

The makers of Formula 409, relying on good competitor analysis, learned of the development. They began to quietly withdraw Formula 409 from stores in the Denver area. Retailers' shipments were delayed, promotion was reduced. This allowed Cinch to succeed very well in the tests and raised Procter & Gamble's hopes for its national introduction of the product.

Just before this introduction, Formula 409 was offered in a special promotion. It wasn't just a price cut—which Procter & Gamble could easily have matched. Rather, customers were offered a drastically reduced price on a 16-ounce bottle plus a half gallon. Many spray cleaner customers were thereby induced to purchase a *six-month supply* of Formula 409. When Cinch hit the market, sales were virtually nonexistent. Expensive promotions had no effect. Prepared for a rush of business after its test results, Procter & Gamble experienced especially heavy losses. Within a year, Cinch was withdrawn from the market.

This guerrilla tactic was an extreme example of the indirect approach. Formula 409's makers had to make sure the test of Cinch was a success—otherwise Procter & Gamble might have formulated an even more effective product introduction, or focused more on Formula 409 as a competitor. It then had to make sure the introduction of Cinch was a total failure. Otherwise, Procter & Gamble might have settled in for a prolonged campaign, with the advantage gradually shifting to a larger company. Timely competitor analysis was needed, followed by adroit maneuvering.

Strategy versus Tactics

In fighting your market "wars," it's always useful to keep in mind the distinction between strategy and tactics. Strategy is *what* you want to achieve, tactics is *how* you plan to achieve it.

For example, you set a strategic goal of gaining a five percent increase in market share this year. It is a mistake to then relay the strategy directly to operating units by requiring each of them to increase their share of a particular market by 5 percent. That's a case of trying to turn a strategy into a tactic. Instead, you should use competitor analysis to focus your sights on competitors' weaknesses and set your tactics accordingly.

For example, suppose your main competitor is having trouble coordinating its marketing plans in the Eastern region. You might focus on this weakness and establish a plan to "gain 15 percent in the Eastern region while holding current market share elsewhere." This may accomplish your strategy of five percent overall market share increase with less difficulty and less cost. Review your strategy and tactics in Competitive Analysis Worksheet 28.

Using Competitor Analysis to Defend Your Market Share

Grandiose plans for market penetration are worth little if a company cannot protect its current market territory. Having looked at ways in which you can turn competitors' weaknesses against them, now consider how they might try to do the same to you—and what you can do to prevent it.

Competitive Analysis Worksheet 29 will focus your attention on some of the aspects of your business that need to be defended. Part A considers important market sectors and also draws your attention to your most serious potential functional weakness. Important market sectors might be key customers, geographic regions, or core businesses. They may be currently under attack or only hold the potential to be.

Establishing a Defensive Position

While mobility and indirect approach are the key aspects of attack, position is the crux of defense. In market competition, this means which areas you choose to defend and how. A well-planned attack by one or more competitors will inevitably have some effect on your market fortunes. You must choose those areas that are most important to you and set up your defenses to ward off attacks against them.

For example, Encore Electrical is a company in the electrical components industry. Its major product areas are connectors and relays. A low-priced competitor from abroad was making inroads into both areas. Encore managers, through their competitor analysis, had a good view of the market and this competitor's capabilities and intentions. They devised a two-part defensive plan:

1. **Connectors.** This sector provides only 27 percent of our operating profits. It is a low-margin, price-sensitive business. Our strategy: to keep competing vigorously in order to make it difficult for the competitor to gain market share, but to make no new investments.

2. Relays. This more profitable sector accounts for a large proportion of our earnings. We need to speed up our investment in product development in order to retain and expand our share of the high-end, value-added segment. At the same time, we should modernize our production facilities in order to cut costs and remain a major factor in the low-end segment.

This is a good defensive plan because it concentrates Encore's resources on the most important sectors without ceding to the competitor easy gains in any area.

Part B of Competitive Analysis Worksheet 29 asks you to define crucial areas of your business. They may not be under attack now, but these will be the areas to watch closely for any competitor moves and to begin thinking about what defenses you might employ.

Preventing Flank Attacks

It's worth noting an aspect of Encore's defensive plan discussed above. The company is not willing to give up a segment of the regulator market even though the low-end products are not the most profitable. It plans to invest in new production processes in order to remain competitive, even though Encore's strengths lie in the value-added sector.

This strategy came about because competitive analysis led Encore managers to study the competitor's thinking. The foreign company's managers reason that gaining a foothold in the cheaper regulators will give them the market opening, the manufacturing experience, and other benefits that will enable them to build into a full-line producer. This is just what Encore wants to avoid.

Therefore, in addition to building on its strengths, Encore must shore up its weaknesses. Otherwise, it will be fighting a losing battle as the competitor steadily encroaches from the low-price flank.

The invasion of the U.S. motorcycle market by Japanese manufacturers, mentioned earlier, is a good example of the danger here. Harley-Davidson, the U.S. producer, conceded the low end of the market.

· ·

Information Key

What would you do if, without warning, a powerful new competitor suddenly began to encroach on your core business? Are you prepared for such an event?

_____

_____

_____

· ·

The Japanese companies developed strong distribution bases from which to gradually move into high-end sectors crucial to the U.S. company.

A better strategy for Harley-Davidson would have been to protect its flank by contesting the low end of the market before the Japanese companies captured it, and at the same time building on its strengths in larger motorcycles.

Planning a Counterattack

Your competitor seeks to gain market share by taking on a new distributor. You reply by adding more salespeople. The competitor steps up its advertising. You counter with coupons and in-store promotions. Counterattack can be the most effective defense because it not only increases the difficulty of a competitor's gains, but throws it off balance as well.

A company that is making a major market move—a new product line, a sales effort, a price cut—is committing itself to a course of action and therefore leaving itself vulnerable to other maneuvers. For example, Encore might have countered its competitor's price tactics by offering free engineering appraisal to potential customers. It could have devised a delivery system that would have cut customers' inventories. It might have extended credit terms for customers. These counterattacks would have disrupted the competitor's plans because they hit its weaknesses rather than just defended against its attacks.

. . . .

Action Probes

If a competitor's tactics require expensive moves on your part, is there a way you can focus or specialize your market approach in order to defend market share more easily?

If a competitor's attack requires that you quickly develop a new product, can you do it through licensing or joint venture, instead of investing heavily in research?

. . . .

Withdrawal

In 1970, General Electric managers conducted a strategic review of several business lines. They questioned their participation in nuclear power, jet engines, and computers. While the company had the resources to pursue all three areas, strategists determined that they had little chance to surpass IBM in computers and that this was the least attractive long-term sector. Their competitor analysis identified Honeywell as the most likely candidate to purchase General Electric's computer assets. A deal was arranged and General Electric left the business with recovery of all its investments.

RCA, on the other hand, decided to remain in the computer business and fight for position. Its efforts failed, and two years later the firm had to give up its computer operations with heavy losses.

Choosing a good position to defend means deciding which territory *not* to defend. Planned withdrawal is important, just as strategic retreat can be crucial in warfare. An army that tries to defend an untenable position can be routed with heavy casualties. A company that invests in ultimately losing operations is wasting assets that could be better employed elsewhere in its business.

The following are a few of the characteristics that mark a sector you may not wish to defend:

You hold a small market share.

Several stronger competitors are fighting for share.

Your segment of the market is marginal.

The market has few growth prospects.

The area is unrelated to your core business.

The segment does not provide a significant portion of your profits.

There are buyers who will purchase your assets connected with the sector.

Use Part D of Competitive Analysis Worksheet 29 to look at areas of your current operations that may fit these criteria. You may not be interested in withdrawing from these sectors now or in the foreseeable future. But it is worth distinguishing those areas you plan to defend with vigor, and those you will abandon if pressed by competitors.

Rely on Strengths

When Procter & Gamble introduced its new Pringles brand potato chip, the company presented a challenge to traditional chip marketers like Frito-Lay and Wise. The move was a well-conceived flank attack. Procter & Gamble didn't try to duplicate the products of its established competitors, but came up with a new item—identically shaped chips made from processed potatoes.

Competitive analysis gave the defenders a good picture of the market battlefield. They didn't try to overextend themselves by attempting to match the new product. Instead, they fell back on the strengths of their own products—their natural character and taste. They emphasized the processed quality of Pringles and the product's alleged inferior taste. As a result, Pringles had a great deal of difficulty penetrating the market.

Don't be too quick to use novel tactics in fighting off a competitive threat. Use Part E of Competitive Analysis Worksheet 29 to reexamine your company's principal strengths. Which would be useful for defending against market attacks? How can you reinforce them in order to meet a competitor's moves?

Goudchaux/Maison Blanche, a large department store chain in New Orleans, is currently preparing to defend its territory against R.H. Macy, Inc., which is planning to open two large stores in the city. Goudchaux does not plan to try to match Macy's merchandising or other retailing techniques. Instead, the firm is going to rely on its strength—superior customer relations backed by such tactics as interest-free credit cards.

COMPETITIVE ANALYSIS WORKSHEET 27

FINDING WEAKNESSES THROUGH INCONSISTENCY

For each of the competitor's fundamental business goals, discuss whether the objective is congruent with a real opportunity and whether the firm has the resources to accomplish the goal. Then point out any potential weaknesses in the plans.

Goal #1: _____

    Opportunity: _____

    _____

    Resources: _____

    _____

    Weaknesses: _____

    _____

Goal #2: _____

    Opportunity: _____

    _____

    Resources: _____

    _____

    Weakness: _____

    _____

Goal #3: _____

    Opportunity: _____

    _____

    Resources: _____

    _____

    Weakness: _____

    _____

COMPETITIVE ANALYSIS WORKSHEET 28

ANALYSIS SHEET: STRATEGY VERSUS TACTICS

List three strategic goals that your company is currently pursuing and briefly describe the tactics you are using to accomplish each.

Strategy: _____

_____

Tactics: _____

_____

Strategy: _____

_____

Tactics: _____

_____

Strategy: _____

_____

Tactics: _____

_____

COMPETITIVE ANALYSIS WORKSHEET 29

ANALYSIS SHEET: TURNING COMPETITIVE ANALYSIS INTO EFFECTIVE MARKET DEFENSE

A. List three market sectors currently under attack by competitors:

Sector	Attacked by	Defense Plan
_____	_____	_____
_____	_____	_____
_____	_____	_____

List three more areas that could potentially come under attack:

_____	_____	_____
_____	_____	_____
_____	_____	_____

In which functions are you particularly weak?

_____

_____

_____

How are your competitors most likely to gain from this weakness?

_____

_____

_____

B. Which sector is most important to your business?

Sector: _____   Percent of sales ____%

Percent of profit ____%

Why important? _____

_____

C. Discuss two current competitive challenges you face and potential counterattacks:

Challenge: _____

Counterattack: _____

_____

Challenge: _____

Counterattack: _____

_____

D. Name two areas of your current operations from which you might withdraw
if pressed by competitors and state your reasons:

Sector: _____ Reason: _____

Sector: _____ Reason: _____

E. Cite the principal strengths of your company which could serve as the first
line in fighting off a competitive challenge:

_____

_____

_____

15

Taking a Look at International Competitive Analysis

In evaluating their competitive situation, most companies first focus on domestic operations and domestic competitors. Business at home is the main concern of a majority of firms, and local rivals usually offer the most immediate and serious competitive threat.

Competitive analysis, though, cannot stop at your nation's borders. In the United States, auto and steel makers were both caught unaware by foreign competition and paid a heavy price for their lack of vigilance. Consider the following indicators of the changing competitive environment:

> Siemens and ITT are both aggressively marketing their telecommunications equipment in almost every country in the world.
>
> Fujitsu has developed a mainframe computer for which it guarantees 99 percent uptime—and plans to use it to compete against IBM worldwide.
>
> Sanyo and Toshiba are both developing lines of appliances with the aim of invading the U.S. market.

These developments represent significant competitive threats that local companies cannot ignore unless they wish to follow in the footsteps of companies like Warwick, Motorola, and Admiral, all of which were driven from the color television market by the crush of foreign competition.

Why International Competitor Analysis Is Essential

The most important economic development over the next 10 years could very well be the increasingly rapid "globalization" of business. This refers to more than just the growing dominance of traditional multinational firms. It means a new definition of markets, new standardization of products, and a rearrangement of economies of scale.

The result: competition that nearly erases national borders. For example, the video cassette recorder has become popular simultaneously in Japan, Europe, and the United States, and has just as quickly spread to Saudi Arabia, Venezuela, and Indonesia. People in all parts of the world drive Mercedes-Benz cars, wear Gucci shoes, and listen to Sony Walkman recorders.

Whole technologies are going global. Robotics, fiber optics, plastics—all are developing in a world environment, not just in one country. Aircraft makers have long sold their products globally in order to amortize the high cost of development. Now the same pressures are affecting automobile companies, pharmaceutical manufacturers, and many others.

Economies of scale are changing. A high-speed modern factory using expensive automation techniques needs world markets to handle the volume of its output and to make it cost effective. Matsushita recently opened such a plant in Singapore to make compressors. It sells the factory's products not only in Asia but in the Middle East, Europe, and the United States. In America, the company's economy of scale has helped it to capture 30 percent of the refrigerator compressor market.

What do these developments mean to you? First, you must begin by examining the status of your own industry. Use Competitive Analysis Worksheet 30 at the end of this chapter to take a look at the globalization of your main product areas. Don't be content if international competition is currently low. Changes can occur practically overnight. Part A asks you to look at all current and potential foreign entrants in your market. Use the same criteria you used for evaluating other competitors and potential competitors.

Part B examines the factors that might attract or repel foreign invaders to your market. And in Part C, look at the competitive advantages that potential entrants would bring to your market and sum up the competitive threat that they pose.

How to Gather Information on International Competitors

Many of the techniques discussed in earlier chapters can be applied to collecting data on international competitors. In some cases, competitor data may be easier to gather in an international arena. For example, Suzuki was able to acquire Toyota test data from a U.S. importer. The information was unavailable in Japan.

When turning to international data collection, keep two factors in mind:

Timeliness. For example, in 1984 a company interested in the phonograph market in Venezuela would have had to rely on 1978 data. Japanese figures on the same market would have dated from 1983. Make sure you are aware of *when* information is compiled so that you don't compare widely dissimilar figures.

Accuracy. Data errors can occur not only because of sloppy statistical work in compiling information, but also because of differences in definitions, standards, measures and data collection techniques. A rating of "superior" might mean different things in different countries. In one part of the world, the "youth market" might mean consumers from ages 8 to 18, while elsewhere it could refer to persons 17 to 30.

Bibliographies

Since you are likely to be even less familiar with useful published sources of information abroad, good bibliographies are essential in directing you to sources you'd otherwise overlook. Some good works to start with:

Sources of Asian/Pacific Economic Information
Sources of African & Middle Eastern Economic Information
available from: Greenwood Press
88 Post Road West
P.O. Box 5007
Westport, CT 06881

Directory of Information Sources in Japan

available from: Maruzen Co., Ltd.
P.O. Box 5050
Tokyo 100–31
Japan

Source of European Economic Information

available from: Gower Publishing Co., Ltd.
Gower House
Croft Rd., Aldershot
Hants GU11 3HR
England

Directories

International directories are useful for finding out who potential competitors are around the world. They can point you toward further information sources: the competitor companies themselves, suppliers, customers, and firms in related industries. Helpful directories include:

Major Companies of the Far East

Graham & Trotman, Ltd.
Sterling House
66 Wilton Rd.
London SW1V 1DE
England

Principal International Business
Europe's 10,000 Largest Companies
Guide to Key British Enterprises

Dun's Marketing Services
3 Century Drive
Parsippany, NJ 07054

Japan Trade Directory
Gale Research Co.
Book Tower
Detroit, MI 48226

Trade Sources

Many trade organizations cross national boundaries. Others may be useful sources of data about competitors' home markets or penetration of other countries. Many trade publications are directed at a world market and contain valuable competitor information. These include:

Canadian Banker
Chemical Week
Euromoney
International Labour Review
International Trade Forum
Journal of Common Market Studies
World Mining

Governmental and Quasigovernmental Sources

Governmental bodies at every level can provide you with both general economic and business statistics and competitor-specific data. Start by inquiring about your area of interest from the national government. Then ask local representatives—subsidiary managers, sales office managers, or distributors—to conduct more detailed research, probing regional and local government bodies.

International organizations are sometimes good sources of general statistics, regional summaries, trade, and political information. Here are a few typical governmental and quasigovernmental sources.

Her Majesty's Stationery Office
P.O. Box 569
London SE 1 9NH
England

European Economic Community
Office des Publications Officielles
5 Rue du Commerce
BP 1003 Luxembourg

Organization for Economic
   Cooperation and Development
2 Rue Andre Pascal
75775 Paris / Cedex 16
France

Saudi Consulting House
P.O. Box 1267
Riyadh
Saudi Arabia

Central Bureau of Statistics
Hakirya
Gwat Ram
Jerusalem
Israel

Private Research Companies

With offices located throughout the world, private research firms can often provide efficient data-gathering services not available to a client company. Use them to investigate important competitors in areas where you lack contacts. A few worldwide firms include:

A.C. Nielsen Co.
Nielsen Plaza
Northbrook, IL 60062

Predicasts, Inc.
11001 Cedar Ave.
Cleveland, OH 44106

FIND/SVP
500 Fifth Ave.
New York, NY 10036

International Market Evaluation

Besides looking at particular companies, your competitor analysis effort should include a broader look at social and economic factors in other nations. This information has a number of uses:

It enables you to examine the home market conditions of foreign competitors. For example, U.S. steel companies know that Japanese producers have a labor rate of $20 per ton compared to the $150 rate in the United States.

It enables you to evaluate country-specific risks associated with your own entry into international markets. For instance, telephone answering machines would not be a widely popular product in the Philippines where only nine percent of the population has phones.

It allows you to identify emerging markets.

It helps you pinpoint areas of low cost manufacturing, or inexpensive sources of supply.

Use Competitive Analysis Worksheet 31 at the end of this chapter to examine some of the risk factors associated with doing business in other countries. Duplicate the page and fill out one copy for each country in which you are interested.

Part A looks at the nation's economic prosperity and will highlight any potential trouble spots such as high inflation, a large foreign debt, or a poor balance of payments. Part B gives some idea of the social situation in the country and its attractiveness as a place to do business.

Part C helps you obtain a brief overview of the political stability of the nation.

Competing Internationally

Companies wishing to compete in international markets face both problems and opportunities. Their experience, skills in marketing or manufacturing, and access to materials or labor may prove to be true competitive advantages in world markets. But burdens ranging from transportation costs to government restrictions will hinder expansion at the same time—not to mention the natural advantages possessed by local competitors.

The first thing to realize as you move from strictly domestic selling or low-level export to actual international competition is that such a move requires rigorous planning, meticulous organization, and adept administration. You will have to remain flexible without losing sight of your basic goals. Astute competitive analysis is a prerequisite for all these facets of your approach.

World Products

Before you can penetrate international markets, you need a product you can sell on a worldwide basis. Clearly you can't develop separate products to suit the conditions of each market. That would eliminate all your economies and diminish any advantage you have over local producers.

Realizing this, more and more companies are aiming for "world products." Here are a few of the strategies they are using to make products more adaptable to international conditions.

1. **Standardize.** Black & Decker cut the number of different motors in its hand tools from 250 to 25. The varieties it retained were selected to suit the conditions of markets around the world. This increased the company's economies of scale and created more adaptable products.

2. **Technology.** Choose a promising technology with wide applications. For example, plain paper copiers have proven to be a powerful world product. Applications of new plastics or fiber optics may gain wide acceptance across borders.

3. **Design.** Another way to achieve a world product is to design one that appeals to a wide variety of different markets. This is the strategy that Caterpillar uses in developing earth-moving equipment. It concentrates on those products that can be used virtually anywhere and avoids specialty items.

4. **Adaptability.** This is Ericsson's strategy in telecommunications equipment. From the early stages of product development, the idea of adapting the item to different conditions is considered. Minor modifications are all that is required to suit it to new markets.

5. **Market.** In some cases an identifiable world market already exists. Canon cameras, for example, are aimed at a particular market segment that crosses national boundaries. Toyota's Corolla and Ford's Escort are both based on similar concepts.

International Efficiencies

Another aspect of international competition is to identify cost savings in the international arena—sources of cheap labor or materials, locations with logistical or regulatory advantages. This consideration has led many companies to try for a competitive advantage by moving operations out of their home countries. For example, Ford now makes tractors in England and Belgium. DuPont has set up plants in France and the Netherlands. BSR moved its operations from England to Hong Kong.

International suppliers may offer cost savings. Ingersoll-Rand closed down its U.S. casting plant when it found that it could purchase the components for half the cost abroad. Goodyear abandoned its export of tires to Asia and purchased a 30 percent interest in the Toyo Tire Co. of Japan.

. . . .

Information Key

Which of your current products would appeal to a world market? Which could be adapted easily for such a purpose? Ask the same questions about the products of your main competitor. How would its marketing of products in international markets affect its competitive advantage (e.g., increase economies of scale)?

Your products: _____

_____

Your competitor's products: _____

_____

_____

. . . .

These types of moves could be useful for your company. You should also keep an eye on competitors' tactics in this area. Are they buying inexpensive textiles in Sri Lanka? Are they moving an electronics assembly operation to Malaysia to cut labor costs?

Labor rate differentials tend to narrow fairly rapidly. Some Japanese companies have moved assets out of cheap labor areas in Southeast Asia and invested them in modern, automated plants at home. As automation affects more and more industries, the advantages achieved in cheap labor diminish. The economies of off-shore production must always outweigh the disadvantages of transportation costs and longer lead times.

Competing in Foreign Markets

Moving into markets in other countries presents special difficulties for a firm accustomed to domestic competition. The following steps are useful for avoiding problems.

1. ***Study the Market.*** Diligent competitor analysis is vital before you plan your move. Look particularly at the competitive advantages of current market leaders. What compensating advantages will you bring to the market? Do you have the resources to match their natural lead in after-market service, customer relations, and manufacturing efficiencies?

2. **Look for Openings.** Daimler-Benz chairman Werner Breitschweidt calls these "white spots on the map," that is, gaps in geographic coverage of an area in relation to a certain product. In-depth competitive analysis has led Daimler-Benz to build a truck plant in Turkey and to plan another in Egypt.

3. **Move Quickly.** Usually a marginal market position is difficult for a foreign firm to maintain. You will be spending to establish a structure in the company (in sales, marketing, etc.) and to introduce your products. To repay these costs, you need to gain a sizable market share quickly.

4. **Transfer Advantages.** Make sure you've carefully analyzed the factors which give you a competitive advantage at home and are ready to employ those factors in your new markets. For example, Japanese companies have been setting up plants in the United States to build everything from subway cars to springs. To make sure they compete effectively, they have been careful to apply the management techniques that have worked for them at home, including attention to the ratio of defective parts to absenteeism, to labor turnover, and to market share dynamics.

5. **Differentiate.** You probably won't be able to profit from foreign markets if your product does not have a clear benefit that appeals to a market segment in the country you are trying to enter. German beer has a definite taste advantage over the product of American brewers, Italian leather goods sell abroad based on styling and workmanship, and Japanese integrated circuit producers distinguish their products by their consistent quality.

6. **Plan Distribution Strategy.** Too many companies neglect a careful analysis of the distribution system in the target market. This has been a major problem for companies trying to sell in Japan. You may want to use distributors who sell your products

. . . .

Action Probes

What mistakes are competitors making in approaching foreign markets? How can you take advantage of this situation in planning your own international marketing?

What advantages would your products enjoy in markets abroad that they don't have at home (e.g., "exotic" appeal, national reputation for quality, technical innovations, etc.)?

. . . .

under their own brand names. Or you may have to turn to different distribution patterns than you use at home.

7. **Shape Your Marketing Effort.** Don't simply transfer domestic marketing techniques to foreign countries. Look at the situation and at how competitors' products are positioned. Here are some examples of targeting marketing efforts.

Varta, a West German company, markets its batteries in Britain with a no-leak guarantee. The purpose is to differentiate them from the market leaders (Duracell and Ever Ready) which both emphasize long life.

Seagram (U.K.) markets Paul Masson wine in England by playing up the product's image as a California wine. It uses distinctive packaging to set it apart from the products of competitors.

Coca-Cola used the theme "Coke is it" in direct competition with Pepsi-Cola in the United States, but dropped the slogan in international markets because it might have been seen as arrogant.

Ford markets its Sierra model in Germany based on its mechanical and technical features. In Italy and Spain, the company emphasizes the car's styling.

Defense Against International Competitors

Defending your current market share against foreign competition is first and foremost a matter of keen competitor analysis—staying

. . . .

Information Key

Take a look at the most important foreign competitor currently participating in your market. How important is its business in your country to the firm? How committed is it to the market?

_____

_____

_____

. . . .

aware of which international companies might begin competing in your territory and of what advantages they bring to the fight.

Don't make the mistake of ignoring foreign competitors until it's too late. Question the extent of the competitor's international stake. Are its foreign markets important? Or only a sideline? Is the company virtually "dumping" goods to fill capacity? Or generating a substantial profit internationally? What portion of its assets are devoted to foreign markets? For example, Eastman Kodak makes only 5.7 percent of its operating income abroad. The company is likely to be an entirely different kind of competitor internationally than is Dow Chemical, which makes 74 percent of its income in foreign markets.

Counterattack

One technique that has proven successful in fighting off international competitors is to attack them in home markets or in other foreign markets. This can disrupt the cash flow they need to expand in your territory. It can deny them manufacturing economies and experience. And it offers potentially profitable areas of operations for your own firm. Consider:

IBM holds 25 percent of the Japanese computer market. This position has slowed down the progress of companies like Fujitsu and Hitachi in their efforts to market computers abroad.

Cincinnati Milicron markets its robotic equipment in Europe and Japan partly to pressure local producers who are considering expanding into Cincinnati Milicron's home market.

General Electric licensed its gas turbine technology to companies in Italy, West Germany, and Japan, giving up direct participation in those markets in order to eliminate potential competitors from the lucrative U.S. market.

COMPETITIVE ANALYSIS WORKSHEET 30

ANALYSIS WORKSHEET: EVALUATION OF INTERNATIONAL COMPETITORS

A. List all foreign and/or multinational companies currently participating in your market sector:

Company	Base Country	Share of This Market	Growth Rate	Participation	
				Local Product	Export
_____	_____	_____	_____	_____	_____
_____	_____	_____	_____	_____	_____
_____	_____	_____	_____	_____	_____

List all foreign and/or multinational companies which could potentially begin competing in your market sector (choose the companies most likely to move into the market):

Company	Base Country	Currently Participates in (Related Markets)	Threat to (Our Market)
_____	_____	_____	_____
_____	_____	_____	_____
_____	_____	_____	_____

B. What factors might attract international competition to your base market?

_____

_____

_____

_____

Why are some foreign competitors not currently participating in the market (e.g., market segment is too small, government restrictions, tariffs, etc.)?

_____

_____

_____

_____

What are the most important barriers to international competitors seeking to enter your market?

_____

_____

_____

_____

C. What special competitive advantages do international companies bring to your market (cheaper sources of labor or materials, technical lead, manufacturing experience, etc.)?

_____

_____

_____

_____

D. Sum up the competitive threat posed by international competitors:

_____

_____

_____

_____

COMPETITIVE ANALYSIS WORKSHEET 31

ANALYSIS SHEET: EVALUATING COUNTRY RISK

Country: _____ Area: _____

Population: _____

A. Economy

Unemployment rate _____ Inflation rate _____

Rate of real economic growth _____

Gross domestic product per capita _____

	Last Year	19__	19__
Total imports	_____	_____	_____
Total exports	_____	_____	_____
Trade surplus (deficit)	_____	_____	_____

Ratio of current account balance to gross domestic product _____

Ratio of exports to *basic* imports (food, energy, spare parts) _____

Are exports diversified? _____ Yes _____ No

Percent of exports accounted for by most important product _____

Foreign debt _____

As percent of gross domestic product _____

B. Social and Business Conditions

Literacy (percent of population) _____

Rating of the Following Aspects:	High	Average	Low
Training and skills of workers	_____	_____	_____
Efficiency of public administration	_____	_____	_____
Attractiveness of business climate	_____	_____	_____
Internal transportation efficiency	_____	_____	_____

Rating of the Following Aspects:	High	Average	Low
Energy availability	————	————	————
Effectiveness of legal system	————	————	————
Expertise of central bank	————	————	————
Capabilities of managers	————	————	————
Technical sophistication	————	————	————

C. Political Conditions

What is the country's record of political stability?

——— Excellent   ——— Good   ——— Fair   ——— Poor

How long has the current government been in power? _____

How long has the current system of government been in effect? _____

What is the role of the political opposition?

_____

_____

Does the country participate in regional economic structures?

——— Yes   ——— No

Explain: _____

_____

Discuss the distribution of wealth in the country. Is it likely to lead to political unrest?

_____

_____

Is there significant likelihood of war or political instability during the next five years?

——— Yes   ——— No

Explain: _____

_____

Use the following space to briefly summarize the attractiveness of the country as a place to do business:

_____

_____

_____

_____

_____

APPENDIX

Every country, region, city, industry, and so forth will have its own particular sources for competitive information. Governments, trade organizations, private research companies—the list is endless.

The names and addresses in this appendix should merely serve as examples of what is available, to give you an idea of the large number of sources that are there for the asking.

If you decide to use any of these, ask for recent publications, catalogs, even further sources. You'll be well on your way to laying the basis for a solid competitive analysis program.

Africa Guide

Middle East Review Co. Ltd., 21 Gold St., Saffron Walden, Essex, England CB10 1EJ

Annual book that includes economic data on individual countries.

Current African Directories

CBD Research Ltd., 154 High St., Beckenham, Kent, England BR3 1EA

Lists other sources of business information about Africa.

New African Development Yearbook

International Communications, 110 East 59th St., New York, NY 10022

Has data on population, agriculture, mining, and so forth, country by country.

Statistical and Economic Information Bulletin for Africa

United Nations Economic Commission for Africa, Africa Hall, PO Box 3001, Addis Ababa, Ethiopia

Published monthly. Includes trend data.

ACP: Yearbook of Foreign Trade Statistics—Statistical Abstract

Commission of the European Communities, Office for Official Publications of the European Communities, CP 1003, Luxembourg 1, Luxembourg

Business Europe

Business International Corp., 1 Dag Hammarskjöld Plaza, New York, NY 10017

Weekly report on business in Europe with attention to marketing.

Consumer Europe

Euromonitor Publications Ltd., PO Box 115, 41 Russell Square, London, England WC1B 5DL

Annual report on major consumer markets including sales, trends, and imports/exports for 12 product categories.

Current European Directories

CBD Research Ltd., 154 High St., Beckenham, Kent, England BR3 1EA

Resource book listing directories and reference books for all European countries.

Economic Bulletin for Europe

United Nations Publications, Room LX 2300, New York, NY 10017

Includes statistics and other economic data.

European Companies

Gale Research Co., Book Tower, Detroit, MI 48226

Resource book listing sources of information.

Europe's 5000 Largest Companies

Dun & Bradstreet, Inc., 99 Church St., New York, NY 10008

Data on industry, sales, exports, employees, assets, profits, and so forth.

European Directory of Business Information Sources and Services

Center for Business Information, 7 Rue Buffon, 75005 Paris, France

Annual book with updates. Source book for data on economics and marketing statistics.

European Marketing Data & Statistics

Euromonitor Publications Ltd., PO Box 115, 41 Russell Square, London, England WC1B 5DL

Jane's Major Companies of Europe

Macdonald and Jane's Publishers Ltd., Paulton House, 8 Shepardess Walk, London, England N1 7LW

Doing Business with Eastern Europe

Business International Corp., 1 Dag Hammarskjöld Plaza, New York, NY 10017

Multiple volumes with updates. One volume for each country. Includes economic and marketing data.

International Market Guide—Continental Europe

Dun & Bradstreet, Inc., Box 3224, Church Street Station, New York, NY 10008

Annual listing of thousands of business firms with some detail.

Sources of European Economic Information

Teakfield Ltd., 1 Westmead, Farnborough, Hampshire, England GU14 7RU

Source book. Provides a guide to over 2,000 other sources of information.

Arabian Yearbook

Kelly's Directories Ltd., Neville House, Eden St., Kingston-upon-Thames, Surrey, England KT1 1BY

Annual report on thousands of businesses on the Arabian peninsula.

Middle East and North Africa

Europa Publications Ltd., 18 Bedford Square, London, England WC1B 3JN

Annual book including statistics on 24 countries.

Middle East Yearbook

International Communications, 110 East 59th St., New York, NY 10022

Annual book with statistical data on Middle East countries.

Australia at a Glance

Australian Bureau of Statistics, Box 17 GPO, Canberra, ACT 2600, Australia

Statistics on population, production, mining, building, and so forth.

Catalogue of New Zealand Statistics

New Zealand Department of Statistics, Mulgrave St. (Private Bag), Wellington, New Zealand

Economic and Social Survey of Asia and the Pacific

United Nations Economic & Social Commission for Asia & the Pacific, United Nations Bldg., Bangkok 2, Thailand.

Annual survey of economic developments, agriculture, industry, and so forth.

Industrial Development News Asia and the Pacific

United Nations Publications, Room LX 2300, New York, NY 10017

Report on industrial development.

Japan Company Handbook

Oriental Economist, 1–4 Hongokucho, Nihonbashi, Chuo-ku, Tokyo 103, Japan

Annual report with data on over 1,000 major Japanese firms.

Small Industry for Asia and the Pacific

United Nations Publications, Room LX 2300, New York, NY 10017

Report on industries in the area.

Statistics—Asia and Australia

CBD Research Ltd., 154 High St., Beckenham, Kent, England BR3 1EA

International Bibliography, Information, and Documentation

R.R. Bowker, 1180 Avenue of the Americas, New York, NY 10036

Quarterly report on United Nations publications.

International Market Guide—Latin America

Dun & Bradstreet, Inc., Box 3224, Church Street Station, New York, NY 10008

Listing of businesses in 33 Latin American countries, with data about their products and finances.

Latin America Annual Review

Middle East Review Co. Ltd., 21 Gold St., Saffron Walden, Essex, England CB10 1EJ

Annual report on economic developments.

Latin American Economy—Economic Survey of Latin America

United Nations Publications, Room LX 2300, New York, NY 10017

Provides statistics and other economic data on Latin American countries.

Annual Survey of Manufacturers

U.S. Department of Commerce, Bureau of Census, Washington, DC 20233

Detailed statistics on U.S. industry.

Canadian Key Business Directory

Dun & Bradstreet, Inc., Box 3224, Church Street Station, New York, NY 10008

Directory listing data about major Canadian companies.

Barclay's Country Reports

Barclays Bank, Group Economic Intelligence Unit, 54 Lombard St., London, England EC3P 3AH

Annual reports on the economies of over 100 countries.

Concise Guide to International Markets

International Advertising Assn., 475 Fifth Ave., New York, NY 10017 U.S.A. Published by Leslie Stinton & Partners, 39a London Road, Kingston-upon-Thames, Surrey, KT2 6ND, England

Book containing extensive data and statistics on marketing in 100 markets throughout the world.

Economic Outlook: Global Report

Bank of America, World Information Services, Dept. 3015, Box 37000, San Francisco, CA 94137

Annual report with data on trends and projections.

Grindlays Bank Reports

Grindlays Bank Ltd., 23 Fenchurch St., London, England EC3P 3ED

Annual report on economic, population, and other trends in 25 countries.

International Marketing Data and Statistics

Euromonitor Publications Ltd., PO Box 115, 41 Russell Square, London, England WC1B 5DL

Book with statistics and other data about marketing in 45 countries around the world.

Ulrich's International Periodicals Directory

R.R. Bowker Co., 1180 Avenue of the Americas, New York, NY 10036

Marketing in Europe

The Economist Intelligence Unit Ltd., 10 Rockefeller Plaza, 12th Floor, New York, NY 10020

Company Publications in Print

McGraw-Hill Book Co., 1221 Avenue of the Americas, New York, NY 10020

Editor: Craig T. Norback

Index

Index